1. The winning design by James Ren

2. James Smithson, painting by Johns, 1816.

"I have yielded…to a conviction that it is in his knowledge that man has found his greatness and his happiness…and consequently that no ignorance is probably without loss to him; no error without evil…"

James Smithson

A PICTORIAL TREASURY
OF THE
SMITHSONIAN
INSTITUTION

BY ROBERT B. WIDDER

CHILTON BOOKS A Division of Chilton Company, Publishers · Philadelphia and New York

All photographs are by the various photography departments of the
Smithsonian Institution except for the following.

Matthew Brady 3

John William Brown 643

Kramer, Miller, Lomden, Glassman 159, 285, 290, 310, 370, 459, 472,
546, 572

National Gallery of Art 375-383

Kjell Sandved 691-696

Robert B. Widder 10-14, 16-21, 23-36, 39-41, 43-46, 58, 62-63, 67-68,
70-72, 84, 97-98, 107, 109, 111, 119-120, 134-145, 147-154,
158, 165, 174-175, 196-200, 216-222, 224-225, 228, 235, 238,
240, 259, 260-261, 267-270, 286-289, 291-307, 309, 312-319,
322-328, 333-362, 366, 371, 374, 396, 409-410, 415-416, 440,
446-455, 473-474, 476, 478-479, 497-502, 509, 511-512, 514-516,
521, 523-524, 526-531, 533-538, 541-545, 547-548,
559-564, 567-569, 571, 573-594, 601, 607, 612, 628-629, 631-638,
640-642, 659-662, 673-678, 687, 689-690

Library of Congress Catalog Card Number 66-23965

Designed by Kramer, Miller, Lomden, Glassman

Manufactured in the United States of America.

CONTENTS

ACKNOWLEDGMENTS

So VAST AND SO varied are the collections of the Smithsonian Institution that each person choosing from among the millions of objects preserved within its walls would arrive at a different and highly individual list of the few hundred "treasures" possible to include within the covers of a book. The objects shown in these pages are chosen from the standpoint of what is exhibited in the many galleries of the various Smithsonian museum buildings, the primary consideration being the interest of the nonspecialist who has no great knowledge in any one of the fields covered. With few exceptions, the objects pictured are, or will be, on display somewhere in the Smithsonian Institution.

The author is greatly indebted to the curators, editors, and especially the exhibit specialists who are responsible for the many exhibits that contain most of the objects pictured in the following pages.

Without the assistance of Miss Carolyn Amundson who did much of the necessary research work, and Mr. Paul Hester, Miss Mildred Widder and Mr. D. Hugh Shields who worked many long hours proofreading and typing, this book could not have been written.

Unless otherwise noted, the photographs are the work of the Smithsonian Photographic Services Division, or by the author.

INTRODUCTION

WITH turrets, crenelated battlements, arched windows with leaded panes, and pointed towers, the main building of the Smithsonian Institution rises on the Washington skyline as the exotic climax to one of the most romantic stories in this nation's history. With the erection of this building, a brilliant Englishman's dream of the castle he longed for and the recognition he fought for so bitterly and never won in his native country, or during his lifetime, was achieved at last. In September, 1965, the institution symbolized by those towers celebrated the two hundredth anniversary of the birth of its founder.

Of its many functions ranging from research and scholarship to the publication of scientific writings, the most tangible and best known to the American people is the institution's collecting, preserving, and exhibiting of the treasures of the nation. This volume presents only a small portion of the treasures preserved for all people to see and study; these precious items number in the millions and constitute the most enduring monument to the memory of James Smithson.

PREAMBLE TO A MUSEUM

The Bequest

"I, JAMES SMITHSON, son of Hugh and Elizabeth... bequeath to the United States of America all my property to found at Washington under the name of the Smithsonian Institution an establishment for the increase and diffusion of knowledge among men."

The words are few, their impact great, but the man behind the words was and is a figure cloaked in mystery, a man who was a true representative of the age in which he lived, an age which in the 1820's was drawing to a close.

In the second decade of the nineteenth century the center of the cultural world was London, a lively, sprawling, cosmopolitan city where the newly constructed facades of the Bank of England, Christ Church, Drury Lane, the Haymarket Theatre and the British Museum were making a vigorous backdrop for the birth struggles of the new era that would be the Industrial Age. The beginning efforts of the infant industries were causing the educated man who was well versed in all phases of science and art to give way to one who would specialize in a single branch of learning. The man who sought the reflection of himself in every aspect of his natural environment was vanishing as machines began to shape the world.

Smithson, a prominent scientist and man of letters, saw the new architectural masterpieces, talked with the great intellects of the day, and yet seems to have been an observer more than a participant in the scene. His thoughts were not on the elegant vital world in which he lived but were turned toward a little out-of-the-way corner of the universe that most of his colleagues must have considered gauche and uncivilized.

The popular notion of America was drawn from the many tales of naked savages and huge beasts, of rough settlements carved from the edge of the wilderness, tales of travelers who mixed fact with fantasy and pictured a backwoods country struggling to maintain a precarious footing on the edge of a sinister and forbidding continent. But commerce across the Atlantic was brisk and the learned man of the time could read and hear many accounts of the raw young nation so recently a colony. A scientist such as Smithson would be able to separate fact from fiction and picture for himself a land of settled communities peopled with men of stature and learning. Such a departure from the popular notion would require a romantic turn of mind, a mind such as the one that analyzed chemically a lady's tear and considered *An Improved Method of Making Coffee* a suitable subject for serious discussion.

Little is known of James Smithson's life but the chief enigma is the spark that kindled his interest in the new American nation. His half-brother had fought with the British army during the American Revolution but it seems unlikely that the accounts of an officer defeated at Concord in 1775 would have led a cultured Englishman to consider the warring colony even a potential seat of learning. But such is his only known contact with the United States.

Perhaps it was the influence of a fellow member of the Royal Society that piqued his interest. Benjamin Thompson, Count Rumford, had been born in Woburn, Massachusetts, and after fighting on the side of the British had sailed for England. Like Smithson he was a scientist and in fact founded the Royal Institution. Smithson was a member of the Royal Society and other scientific groups. These men, both in London during the same nine year period and traveling in the same scientific circles, surely must have met. Rumford's "Enquiry Concerning the Source of Heat Which Is Excited by Friction" would have interested Smithson whose "Some Improvements in Lamps" would not have escaped the Count's attention.

If these two gifted scientists did meet, the infant United States in all its aspects would have been a topic of discussion. And who but a man born on the very soil could have given a truer account of the new Republic? Count Rumford, as Benjamin Thompson, had lived in Massachusetts and knew Boston as the cultural center of the new continent. Such a man would have drawn a far different picture of the new country, a picture that would have caused a scientific mind as competent as Smithson's to grasp the vast potential that lay untapped in the young nation's grasp. Count Rumford himself was a living example of what that land could produce.

Whatever the reason, James Smithson looked westward across the ocean with great vision. Having been denied his birthright in his own country he decided to establish his name and further his ambitions and desires in an unknown land. This he did when on the twenty-seventh of October, 1826, he wrote his will and bequeathed his entire fortune to a nation he never visited.

On that October day a great and powerful idea was conceived, a germ that was to grow and flourish into a mighty force. But with great wisdom Smithson spelled out only the name of the institution and its location and stated its objectives in only the broadest of terms, leaving the interpretation and procedure to others. Thus, the brilliant men of the eras to come would be able to mold the institution and shape it to serve best the changing nation and its people.

The Founding

BUT NOT all the leaders of the country were as wise as their benefactor. Objections to accepting tainted British money were raised in Congress, and the cry was heard against the insidious infiltration of English influences. For over seven years acceptance of the bequest was endlessly debated. There was fear that the sovereignty of the United States would be compromised. It was July 28, 1835, before calmer minds, guided by the commonsense arguments of John Quincy Adams, prevailed and Congress accepted the bequest. Thus was born the Smithsonian Institution. Another ten years were to pass before the statesmen could agree on what form the institution was to take.

On August 29, 1838, eleven boxes of English gold sovereigns arrived at the port of New York aboard the *Mediator*. Several days later the gold was recoined into $508,318.46 of American money at the mint in Philadelphia, a sum which would be the equivalent of two and one quarter million dollars today. President Van Buren announced to Congress the receipt of the money and reminded them of their obligation to fulfill the terms of the will, but with such influential statesmen as John C. Calhoun against even the acceptance of the bequest, that task was not easy.

Former President John Quincy Adams was made chairman of the committee to study the problem of the form of the new institution. He favored the creation of an astronomical observatory and was much against the prevailing idea of endowing a university. A senator by the name of Asher Robbins must be credited with first stating what was to prove to be the germ of the idea later adopted, when he suggested "an institution of which there is no model either in this country or in Europe, to provide such a course of education and discipline as would give to the faculties of the human mind an improvement far beyond what they afterwards attain in any of the professional pursuits." The problem remained unsolved until 1846 when President Polk signed the bill officially creating the Smithsonian Institution. Before the end of that year the first Board of Regents had met and elected Joseph Henry secretary.

The First Secretary

THE NEW YORKER who was to direct the new institution was a scientist of international renown. As a youngster he had not been especially studious but had toyed with the idea of becoming a professional actor. Such thoughts had vanished when a book on astronomy and chemistry kindled his interest and caused him to devote his life to the study of the natural sciences.

He became a teacher at Albany Academy where he conducted scientific experiments, and it was here he invented the electromagnetic machine which in 1831 was used at Penfield Ironworks, Crown Point, New York, to separate iron and steel from brass and copper, the first known use of electricity in industry.

In Albany and later at Princeton he experimented with an electromagnetic telegraph. It is possible that he actually invented the telegraph eight years before Morse patented it but did not take out a patent himself because he believed that scientists should be dedicated to pure research and not concern themselves with the commercial and financial bene-

4. Joseph Henry, first secretary of the Smithsonian Institution.

fits of that research. Experiments conducted during his ten years at Princeton contributed greatly to the scientific knowledge of electricity and its uses.

Henry never patented his findings and often was lax in publishing his experiments, thus making it impossible to credit him with several revolutionary discoveries that might have been his. He pursued knowledge for its own sake and let others find practical uses for the fruits of that knowledge.

The first job of the secretary was to formulate a plan of organization. He proposed that the institution encourage research by establishing grants for a program of scientific investigation and by publishing the findings of this and other research in the *Smithsonian Contributions to Knowledge* and other periodical reports. The first of these was entitled *Ancient Monuments of the Mississippi Valley,* a pioneer work in American archaeology which proved an illustrious beginning for the new enterprise.

The act of Congress establishing the Smithsonian Institution had specifically mentioned a library, an art gallery, and a museum. Much of the original library is now housed for safekeeping in the Library of Congress under the name Smithsonian Deposit, although an effective scientific library has always been part of the institution's facilities.

An immediate home for these activities was a pressing need.

The Renwick Building

IN THE LIGHT of present-day Washington it is difficult to realize that the selection of the south portion of the Mall between Seventh and Twelfth Streets was greatly criticized for being too remote from the city and in an unsavory part of town. The land lay south of the old rundown canal, with the only access to it four very poor wooden bridges. The overgrown area was used by military encampments and for traveling shows and circuses.

As a result of the dissension another spot was designated but difficulties proved too great and finally the Smithsonian Reservation was established on the Mall.

The first plan for the Smithsonian home was introduced in the Senate in 1844 when a maximum of $80,000 was appropriated for a building which was to be plain and durable, without unnecessary ornament. Two years later another bill was introduced, with only the cost changed to $242,129, the exact amount of the interest that had accrued on the money of the Smithson bequest. A large and handsome building was then possible.

Thirteen plans were submitted in open competition, the design by James Renwick, Jr., being selected. The building committee justified their choice of that design in the style of a twelfth-century Norman castle as being completely func-

5

5. Electromagnet, invented by Joseph Henry.

6. Early photograph of Washington showing the Smithsonian Institution in the distance. In the foreground is Fifteenth Street, with sections of columns for the Treasury building lying on the ground.

tional, modern in every aspect, and well adapted to the needs of the growing establishment.

The building was built of Seneca Creek freestone from the Bull Run Quarry, twenty-three miles from Washington. This type stone is said to be comparatively soft when first quarried, lending itself to carving, becoming harder over the years and able to withstand weather and long usage. The building and the cost were spread over five years, about $236,000 having been spent at the end of that time. Masonic ceremonies were held for the laying of the cornerstone, the grand marshall using the same gavel and apron as were used by George Washington in laying the cornerstone of the Capitol building.

In its earliest years the building not only housed the institution but its staff members as well. Joseph Henry and his wife and four children lived in the east wing from 1855 until his death twenty-three years later. As other scientists and curators joined the staff they were given living quarters, particularly in the tower rooms of the building, especially if they had no family.

The Creation of a National Museum

THE FIRST EFFORTS toward a national museum did not begin with the Smithsonian Institution. Charles Willson Peale is credited with founding the first public museum in America in 1785. Although other cities soon had museums of their own, Peale's Museum in Philadelphia seems to have been the unofficial national museum. The Patent Office, which was fondly known as the American Museum of Arts, displayed models of inventions. Thomas Jefferson's collections of fossilized bones were deposited in the Peale Museum, as were materials, scientific and natural, that had been collected in the Northwest Territory by Lewis and Clark, and the results of other important government sponsored expeditions.

In 1840 the National Institution for the Promotion of Science was founded, taking over from the defunct Metropolitan Society, the first society of its kind in the city of Washington. The National Institution, later known as the National Institute, was named custodian of James Smithson's collection of minerals. The membership of the Institute included many prominent statesmen who were influential in gathering together the collections of natural history, ethnology, and related objects. A large portion of the Patent Office building was turned over to the Institute. The date given for the establishment of the United States National Museum is 1842.

It was not until 1857 that the new Smithsonian building was ready to house a museum. With the National Cabinet of Curiosities transferred from the Patent Office, to be followed four years later by the collections of the National Institute, which was then disbanded, the United States National Museum became an important part of the Smithsonian Institution.

6

7

UNITED STATES NATIONAL MUSEUM

8

7. The first gold nugget, found by James W. Marshall at Sutter's Mill, California.

8. Varieties of Smithsonite.

9. Early drawing of the interior of The United States National Museum.

J AMES SMITHSON, the scientist, first identified and analyzed zinc carbonate, which was named smithsonite in his honor. His cabinet of minerals, although later lost in the great fire, was the beginning of the present-day collection of gems and minerals, one of the finest and most complete in the world.

A survey of man's knowledge as indicated by the items displayed in the United States National Museum can have no better beginning than with the earth beneath the feet of the American people. The geological make-up of the North American continent has contributed greatly to the character and prosperity of the nation. The shape, size, and number of the United States were greatly influenced by a fragment of gold about the size of a cornflake, documented as the first nugget found by James W. Marshall at Sutter's Mill, which led to the madness and fever known as the California Gold Rush. This bit of metal was given to the United States Army by the man who found it and at present resides in the Hall of Gems and Minerals.

9

Only a small portion of the thousands of minerals in the collection are on view there, but they make an impressive eye-catching and beautiful display, as well as demonstrating vividly the marvelous complexity of this continent.

The Smithsonian Institution, in its efforts to increase and diffuse knowledge, appointed Spencer Fullerton Baird as assistant secretary and put him in charge of organizing and directing the museum function of the Institution. Baird had always been a student of natural history. As a young man he had worked with John James Audubon, who had asked him to collect small mammals for use in the preparation of the book, *Quadrupeds of North America.*

When Baird came to Washington in 1850 he brought with him the skins of over five hundred species of American birds, with a thousand eggs and nests, the skins of most of the mammals of the eastern United States, five hundred jars and barrels of specimens of reptiles, fish, and other sea and fresh water creatures, and a large number of skeletons and fossil bones of larger animals. Baird, the second secretary of the Institution, has often been called the father of the National Museum.

Assistant Secretary Baird shaped the United States National Museum and his ideas guided its beginnings. Baird decided not to duplicate other museum collections but to concentrate on areas untouched by others. He thought the museum should be a place where the casual visitor could gain knowledge and the serious student might study.

He proposed that the museum obtain a collection in six ways: by deposits by the government, deposits by individuals, exchanges, purchases, employment of collectors, and donations. Three years later he was able to report that the collections had risen from nothing to the first rank among American cabinets.

GEMS AND MINERALS

THE BROOKLYN BRIDGE and the Gems and Minerals Collection have one thing in common—both are built on foundations begun by one man, Washington A. Roebling. He almost achieved his lifelong goal when, at his death, he had acquired all but twelve of the minerals known at that time.

The answer to the question, "What is a mineral?" is explained in detail and illustrated, with many examples of the various types, in the Hall of Gems and Minerals in the Natural History Building of the Smithsonian Institution. The fluorescence of minerals is clearly shown as the stones move out of black light into visible light before one's eyes. Metals, oxides, oxysalts, silicates, and other types of rock are displayed, with innumerable samples. The Gem Room and the Jade Room in the hall look like fantastic Arabian Nights treasure vaults, with the Hope Diamond the best known among the fortune in jewels on display.

Public spirited donors such as Roebling, Isaac Lea, and Frederich A. Canfield have been greatly responsible for making this collection the world's finest.

Unsuspected beauty and wealth have come to light because of man's constant probing into the Mineral Kingdom that lies beneath his feet. Gold, diamonds, and precious stones are part of the wealth, but so also are coal, petroleum, salt, iron, gypsum, and the common but vitally necessary minerals that support our modern society.

Twenty-five percent of all the known minerals are silicates of one kind or another, and they make up more than 90 percent of the earth's crust. Composed of silicon and oxygen with a scattering of other elements, silicates are of six types, whose characteristics are determined by the way the silicon and oxygen atoms are linked.

The most common of all minerals is quartz, one of the silicates. Sand and gravel are quartz, as are some of the components of granite and sandstone.

10

11

12

13

14

15

16

10. Goethite: iron hydroxide stalactites. Germany.

11. Stalactites, one of the beauties of the underground world, are these strange formations that are suspended from the roofs of limestone caves.

12. Calcite: calcium carbonate. Lavender crystals with chalcopyrite. Joplin, Missouri.

13. Uranite: uranium oxide. Black masses with alteration products. Ruggles Mine, Grafton, New Mexico.

14. Variscite: hydrous aluminum phosphate. Large polished slab. Fairfield, Utah.

15. Opalized wood, oak replaced by opal, from Idaho.

16. Calcite "sand crystals."

17

18

19

20

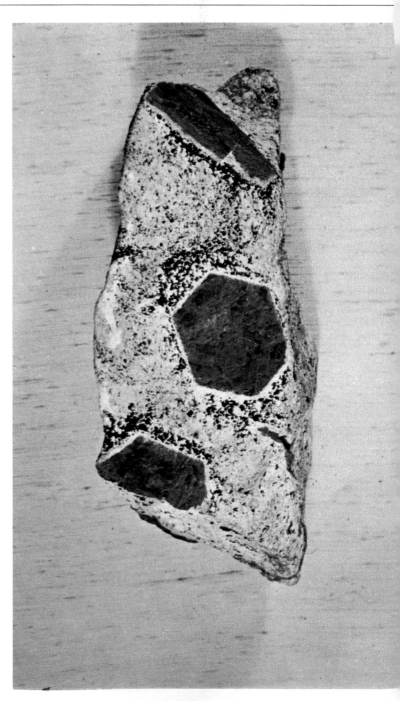

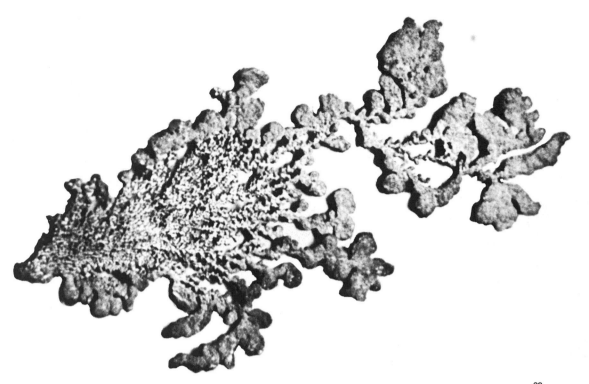

17. Large mass of copper crystals, from Arizona.

18. Wulfenite, lead molybdate, is an oxysalt highly prized by collectors.

19. Bournonite altering to bindheimite, from Austria.

20. Autunite: hydrous calcium uranium phosphate. Large exceptionally fine crystals from Washington.

21. Millerite: nickel sulfide.

22. Corundum: aluminum oxide, ruby crystals in matrix, from Tanzania.

23. Fernlike group of small copper crystals.

24. Unusual malformed copper crystals, from Australia.

23

24

The Faces and Forms of Copper

So COMPLEX is the rock structure and make-up of the earth that any one element can appear in myriad forms, all very different to the eye. For example, almost one hundred forms of copper are on display in the hall yet these are only a small portion of those existing in the earth.

Since metals are very active and combine readily with many other substances, copper appears in pure crystal form and in many combinations. Two of these through the ages have been valued for their beauty, malachite and turquoise. Copper itself is almost the first mark of civilized man because it was probably the first metal to be worked into tools and ornaments in primitive societies. The life force of our electrical society of today flows through endless strands of copper.

25

25. Branching distorted copper crystals, from Michigan.

26. Calcite stalactite colored with copper, from Arizona.

27. Manganese ore: pyrolusite, from Canada.

28. Large distorted isometric copper crystals, from Michigan.

29. Cuprite: copper oxide. Inclusions in calcite, Arizona.

30. Aurichalcite: zinc copper hydroxy-carbonate. Crust of small greenish crystals, Utah.

31. Chalcopyrite: copper iron sulfide, bronze colored crystals on dolomite, from Missouri.

32. Malachite, from Arizona.

18

29

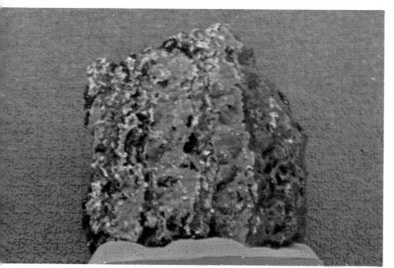

30

31

32

33

33. Pyrite: iron sulfide, from Colorado.

34. Malachite, section showing layers as deposited, from the Republic of the Congo.

35. Chalcopyrite: copper iron sulfide, on dolomite.

36. Paramelaconite: copper oxide, large fine crystals, from Arizona.

37. This necklace of 47 principal diamonds weighing approximately 275 carats was given by Napoleon Bonaparte to his second wife, the Empress Marie Louise, to mark the birth of their son in 1811. The setting is gold and silver and the pendants are removable.

34

35

36

20

ALTHOUGH MOST of them are not in settings, the collection of gem stones in the U. S. National Museum may be considered the "crown jewels" of the United States. Besides such famous stones as the blue colored Hope Diamond and the exquisite sapphire "Star of Asia," are the cameos, jade carvings, alexandrite—the gem that is green in natural light and red when seen in artificial light—and the first man-made diamonds.

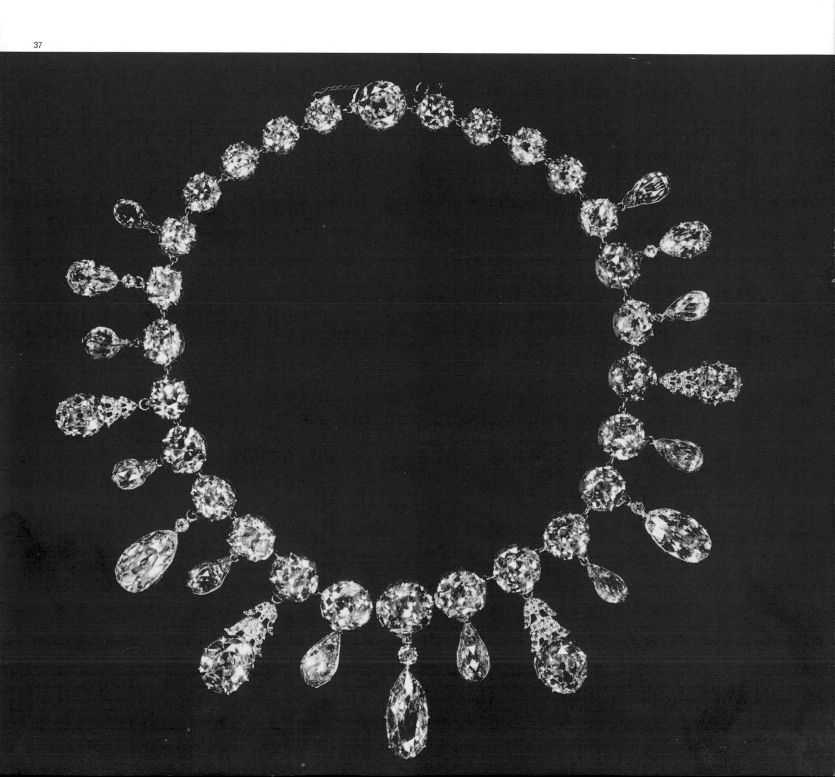

38

39

40

43

4

4

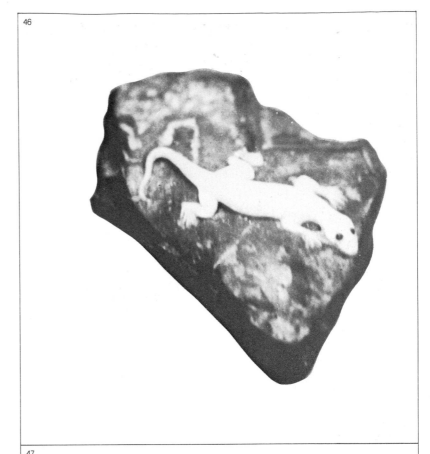

38. The Hope Diamond, the largest of all blue diamonds, 44½ carats, is slightly lopsided, probably due to the bottom part of the tear-drop shape having been cut away so that the original stolen jewel could not be identified. The setting is a circlet of smaller white diamonds on a chain of diamonds.

39. Diamond, curved octahedron in kimberlite, from South Africa.

40. Star sapphire, 330 carats, called the "Star of Asia."

41. Kunzite, 880 carats, from Brazil.

42. Sapphires are a variety of corundum. These are from Montana.

43. Sunstones, from Norway.

44. Moss agate, from Montana.

45. The Portuguese Diamond is 127.01 carats.

46. Opal salamander.

47. Crystallized gold from California.

48. Opals come in many colors ranging from white to black. Collection of white, fire, and black opals from Mexico and Australia.

METEORITES

MAN'S FIRST encounter with outer space came when he examined something he saw fall from the sky and found it to resemble a rock. The oldest known meteorite was seen to fall in France on November 16, 1492. Of the stony type, it weighed 127 kilograms. The Smithsonian meteorite collection, which contains a small piece of it, numbers thousands of many types and is the largest collection in the United States. The study of meteorites may help to solve some of the many problems of space travel.

49. From Clovis, New Mexico, this bronzite chondrite meteorite was the seventh largest in the world of the stony type when discovered in 1961. The curved surface was the leading face during its fall.

50, 51. Shown are two pieces of the Cumberland Falls (Kentucky) Meteorite, a very rare type, made up of two unlike materials from separate sources. The dark portions shown in the cross section contain both metallic inclusions and chondrules; the light portion is free of chondrules. The cut surface is about five inches in length.

25

52

53

54

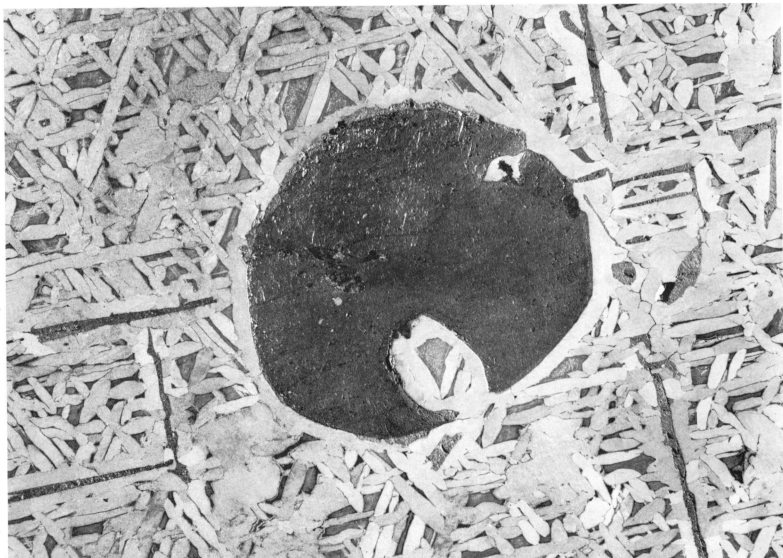

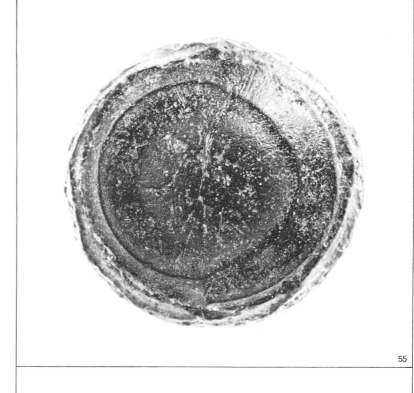

55

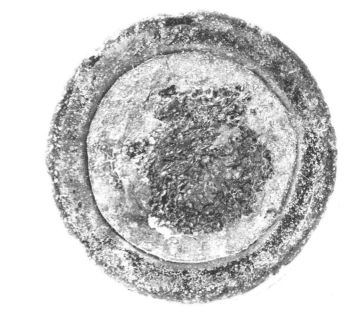

56
57

52, 53, 54. The pointed face of the Grant Meteorite, an iron type originally weighing 1,060 pounds, has a conical form because it fell through the atmosphere in a fixed position. A cross section through the meteorite shows the interior structure. The round dark bodies (one is shown greatly enlarged) are troilite, an iron sulfide rarely found except in meteorites. The long rods are schreibersite, iron nickel phosphide, an even rarer mineral.

55. The front, or leading surface, of this rare glassy tektite pointed forward during its fall. Shown greatly enlarged, it actually measures about ¾ inch in diameter.

56, 57. The back surface of the same tektite is shown. Above is the tektite as it originally appeared; below, smoked to make the surface features more distinct.

27

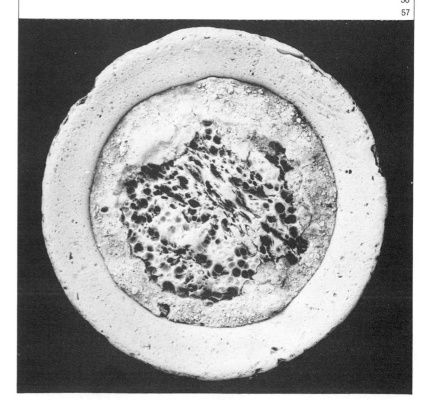

58

FOSSILS

THE STUDY of the types and composition of minerals and meteorites is only the beginning of the fascinating story to be found beneath the earth's surface. The earliest evidence of life itself, the only record existing of millions of creatures now extinct, and the clues to the ancestry of mankind, are to be found imprinted in rock. Thomas Jefferson was once criticized by people who thought the President of the United States should not believe that a rock he found in Virginia was the fossil remains of a prehistoric mastodon. His collection of minerals and fossils was housed in the National Cabinet of Curiosities and the Peale Museum in Philadelphia.

58. The human race has been on earth only a moment compared to the age of the oldest fossil yet discovered. Over one and a half billion years old, this bit of gunflint chert from northern Ontario holds evidence of primitive plant life. Above is a photo enlargement of the fossil.

59. One of the great fossil discoveries of all time was made in 1910 when Charles Doolittle Walcott, fourth secretary of the Smithsonian, found fossils in the shale northeast of Burgess Pass in British Columbia. In the mid-Cambrian sedimentary deposit, 500 to 600 million years old, were marine animals, *Olenoides serratus Romiger*, so well preserved that their highly complex anatomy, including soft parts, can be studied in detail. These ancient crustaceans are shown approximately life size.

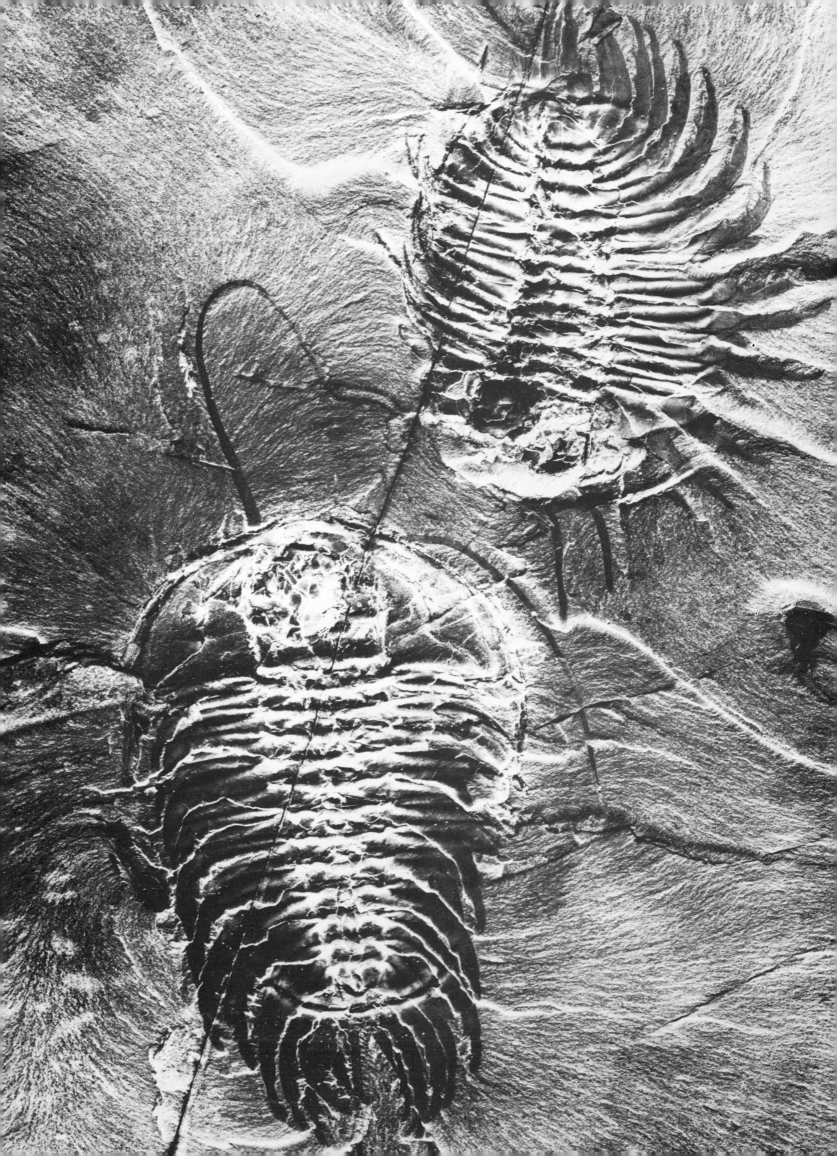

60. On the black mud bottom of the Cambrian Sea that 500 million years ago covered what is now most of the United States, flat-bodied trilobites swim among jellyfish, organ-pipe and pin-cushion sponges, and shrimplike arthropods. The reconstructions of these plants and animals are based on fossil evidence found in rocks of the period.

61. Invertebrates such as ammonites, clams, and snails living in the Cretaceous seas of 125 million years ago closely resemble those of the present day. The site of this sandy mud bottom is now just east of Memphis in western Tennessee.

62. A block of limestone from New York contains large trilobites which, in Ordovician times, 430 to 350 million years ago, were at the peak of their existence.

63. This modern crinoid or sea lily is similar to those of the Mississippian period.

64. Red and white crinoids rise above starfish on the sandy mud bottom of a Mississippian period sea of 255 million years ago in a spot which is now northwestern Indiana.

65. Western Texas was a patch reef underwater in the Permian period, 205 million years ago.

62

63

64

65

Although fossils as evidence of life in prehistoric time may be the imprint of a foot or the contours of a burrow, most often they occur when the organic remains of a living thing are changed to an inorganic mineral through some natural force such as pressure of overlying rock. After millions of years of lying protected by rock itself, the outline of the once living organism is exposed to view by earthquake or erosion or by the work of scientists.

Also of interest are the many types of fake fossils, some manufactured by unscrupulous humans but many resulting from natural processes. Ranging from silicified grass seeds to skeletons of giant reptiles, fossils are the endlessly fascinating clues in one of nature's most complex puzzles.

71

66. In the foreground is the stump of a giant club moss. In the case on the right is an Aneurophyton trunk, the type of plant that made up the first forest in geological history.

67. This polished section of a petrified fern trunk is about eighteen inches in diameter.

68. Knowledge, skill, and luck are needed to find a fossil such as this palm, which includes the apex of the trunk and six leaves, found in Verona, Italy.

69. Echinoderms are marine animals with tube feet for walking, such as starfish and this squidlike Uintacrinus of the Mesozoic period.

70. Angiosperms or flowering plants are of two groups. This fern trunk is of the monocots group.

71. Water scorpions, some of which grew to six feet in length and were the largest of all arthropods, are all now extinct. Pterygotus from the Silurian period of New York.

72

73

72. This Cretaceous monster, Pachydiscus, measuring about four feet across, was found in Montana.

73. One of the herrings of the Age of Mammals in the Cenozoic period was the *Diplomystus dentatus*.

74. The *Heliobatis radians*, a shark-like ray fish of Cretaceous times, lived in fresh water.

75. Shown is a Priscacarum of the Age of Mammals.

76. A typical fish of the Age of Reptiles was the *Lepidotus elvensis*.

77. The extinct marine turtle, *Protostega gigas*, used its legs as oars. This skeleton is about six feet from nose to tip of tail.

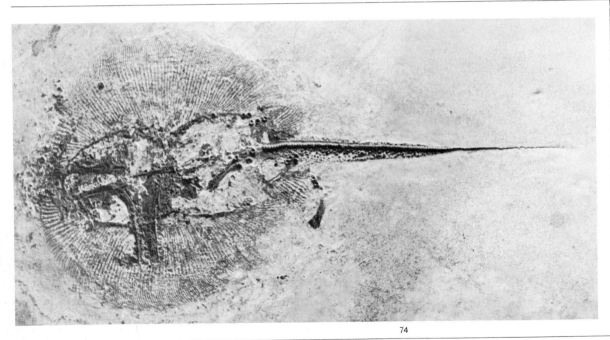

74

76

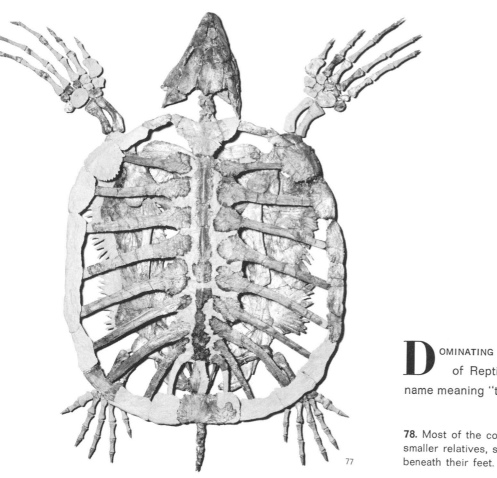

DOMINATING the Halls of Fossils as they dominated the Age of Reptiles, at least in size, are the dinosaurs, the name meaning "terrible lizard."

78. Most of the common dinosaurs, mounted here over their smaller relatives, seem to leave foot marks in the rock beneath their feet.

79. The smaller of these two plant-eating dinosaurs, *Camptosaurus browni,* shows that not all animals of this type were giants.

80. The skeleton of the sauropod dinosaur, Camarasaurus, is shown in the position in which the animal died. Some of its bones had been washed away by water and have been restored.

81. The armored dinosaur, *Stegosaurus stenops,* was found in Wyoming. Similar in appearance and closely related to it is the much smaller *Brachyceratops montanensis* which may represent an ancestral type. The relative length of the hind limbs indicates that they were probably derived from an ancestor which walked on two legs.

82. The *Ceratosaurus nasicornis* was the most common flesh-eating dinosaur of the Jurassic period.

83. This flesh-eater, *Gorgosaurus libratus,* stood six or seven feet high at the hips and was probably fast moving despite its bulk. The distortion of the neck, caused by shrinkage of the soft tissues as they dried, indicates that the animal died on dry land, but because the bones are in their correct relationship, burial by flooding must have occurred soon after death.

84. An aquatic reptile of the Triassic period was the Phytosaur which resembled the crocodile in appearance and habit but was not closely related. The long slender jaws and rows of teeth suggest that it was a fish-eater.

83

84

37

This dinosaur from the Late Cretaceous of Alberta, Canada, was a flesh-eater related to the Jurassic Ceratosaurus. With his strongly clawed, birdlike feet and fearful jaws and teeth, Gorgosaurus must have been a savage and dangerous beast of prey. He stood 6 or 7 feet high at the hips, and, since the lower segments of his hind limbs are longer than his thigh, he must have been fast-moving and active despite his bulk.

The skeleton is mounted as it lay in the rock. Distortion of the neck and tail is primarily due to the shrinking of soft tissues as they dried, indicating that the animal died on a dry surface. But, since nearly all of the bones lie in a proper relationship—thereby indicating that decay took place after burial—burial by flood-carried deposits must have taken place shortly after death.

Anatosaurus is a typical duck-billed dinosaur. So named because of the characteristic flattening and elongation of the front teeth, the duckbills were plant-eaters in which the back teeth had become modified to grinders, a very new development among reptiles. They were wading animals which habitually walked on their hind legs, although they probably walked on all fours at times, perhaps while feeding.

This skeleton from Wyoming is remarkably well preserved and is essentially in the position in which the bones were found.

85

86

85. A typical duck-billed dinosaur, *Anatosaurus annectens,* was a plant-eater whose back teeth had become modified as grinders, rare among reptiles. The bones are displayed in the position in which they were found.

86. The flying reptile *Pteranodon ingens* had wings that were membranes supported by the very long bones of the fourth finger. The reptile soared rather than flapped its wings, as is indicated by the proportionately small wing muscles. The three clawed fingers on the leading

edge of the wings were used for support when at rest. The restoration of the flying reptile is shown.

87. The horned dinosaur, *Triceratops prorsus,* lived during the Upper Cretaceous period and represents one of the last of the dinosaurs.

88. The mosasaurs, large sea reptiles closely related to the modern lizard, swam by means of their long powerful tails. Shown are the skeleton and a small model of the *Tylosaurus proriger.*

88

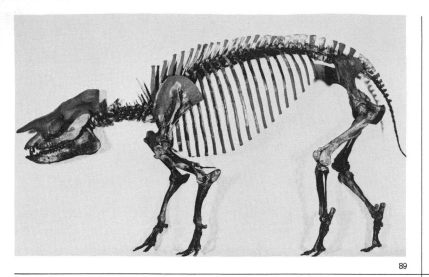

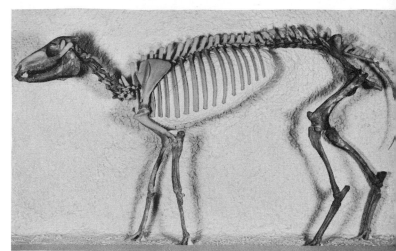

89

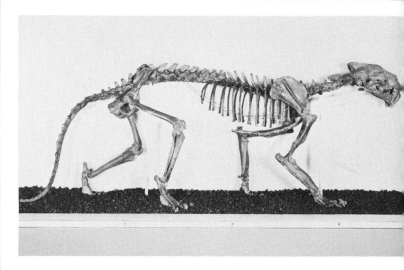

91

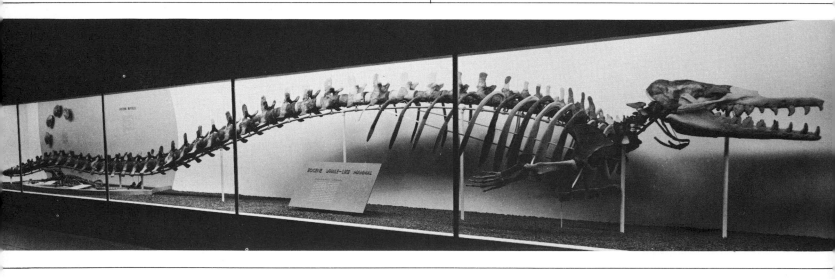

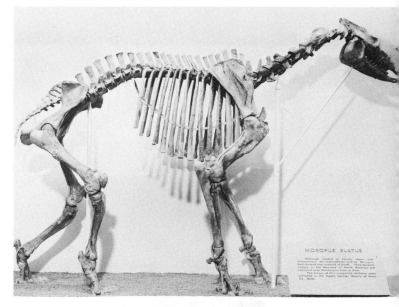

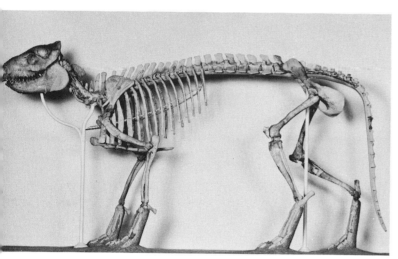

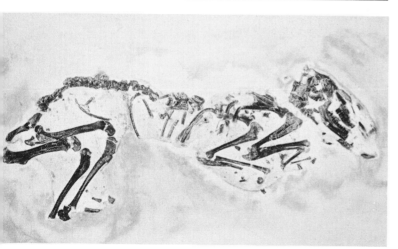

95

96

W ITH THE extinction of the dinosaurs, mammals began to come into their own. About eighty million years ago, in the Paleocene epoch, many groups and species began to emerge and cover widespread areas of the earth.

89. The *Palaeosyops paludosus* lived in Wyoming in the Eocene epoch.

90. The Mesohippus was a type of horse of the Oligocene period.

91. A small deerlike animal closely resembling the South Asian mouse deer was the *Hypertragulus calcaratus.* This partially restored skeleton was found in South Dakota.

92. Easily recognized as a saber-toothed cat, the *Hoplophoneus robustus* was found in the Big Badlands at Cheyenne River, South Dakota.

93. The sixty-foot long skeleton of an Eocene whale-like mammal, *Basilosaurus Cetoides,* found near Coca, Alabama.

94. The *Moropus elatus* was related to the horse and the rhinoceros.

95. A Merycoidodon Gracilis type skeleton is mounted with the bones in their proper places. These animals had many points of resemblance to pigs and herded together like sheep.

96. The milk teeth and the separation of the ends of the long bones indicate that this primitive horse, *Orohippus Pumilus,* died before it was full grown. The fossil is shown as it was found.

41

BIRDS

IN THE 140 million years since the first known true bird, the Archeopteryx, flew above the Jurassic landscape, birds have spread to all parts of the globe. From the smallest, the hummingbird, to the largest, the ostrich, birds have evolved and specialized, adapting themselves to life on the sea, and in the desert, the mountains, and the tropics, and are the only warm blooded inhabitants of the interior of Antarctica.

Since birds have a delicate, lightweight skeletal frame adapted to flight but not easily preserved, very few fossils have been found to show their development from reptiles.

Birds were one of the special interests of Spencer Fullerton Baird, the second secretary of the Institution, the life work of Alexander Wetmore, the sixth secretary, and are the specialty of S. Dillon Ripley, the eighth and present secretary.

97

98

97. Representative of the specimens of rare birds collected by S. Dillon Ripley, present secretary, are top left, the kingfisher, *Sauromarptis gaudichaud;* center, the most splendid longtail, a bird of paradise, *Astrapia splendidissima;* and the crowned pigeon, *Guara cratati minor,* at the bottom.

98. Collected by Spencer Fullerton Baird, second secretary of the Smithsonian Institution, this Baltimore oriole is on display in the Hall of Historic Americans in the Museum of History and Technology.

99. The male argus pheasant clears a space in which it can display its beautiful spread of tail feathers while courting the female. It inhabits the tropical vegetation of Thailand.

100. An inspiration to king, painter, sculptor, and potter, the beautiful peacock courts its female with its fan of tailfeathers, the most elaborate of all bird displays. The long "train" is not a true tail but just supports the glittering plumes.

THE SMITHSONIAN INSTITUTION made a giant step forward in its efforts to increase and diffuse knowledge when Joseph Henry appointed Spencer Fullerton Baird as assistant secretary and put him in charge of organizing and directing the museum function of the institution. As a boy Baird had been a student of natural history and had assembled a large collection of fossils, birds, plants, and mammals found around his Pennsylvania home. As a young man he had worked with James Audubon who asked him to collect small mammals for use in the preparation of the book, *Quadrupeds of North America,* which was to be a companion piece to his famous folio on birds.

When Baird came to Washington in 1850 he brought with him the skins of over five hundred species of American birds with a thousand eggs and nests, the skins of most of the mammals of eastern United States, five hundred jars and barrels of specimens of reptiles, fish and other sea and fresh water creatures, and a large number of skeletons and fossil bones of larger animals. Baird, the second secretary of the institution has often been called the father of the National Museum.

101

103

105

106

107

101. Birds are the only warm-blooded creatures living in the interior of the Antarctic continent. The majestic emperor penguin and the smaller Adelie penguin flourish in this land of eternal ice and snow. Penguins walk upright or travel as the bird in the foreground is doing, tobogganing on its stomach. The bird on the right is the black-backed kelp gull.

102. The death of Martha, the last passenger pigeon, rendered the species extinct.

103. In courtship the sacs on the neck of the sage grouse are inflated, the tail is spread, and the peculiar feathers of the abdomen and sides of the nape are erected.

104. The national bird of Argentina is the ovenbird, which builds its nest of clay in the shape of an oven.

105. The hen hatches and protects her young with the heat of her body.

106. Palm chats live in colonies as shown in this life group.

107. The riflebird of Australia often lines its nest with cast-off snake skins.

45

108. Wallace's standard wing has four erected white plumes on its wings and its spread green gorget bowed forward.

109. An unusual bird is the great crested grebe.

110. After the female of the rhinoceros hornbill lays her eggs in a tree, the male walls her up until the young are old enough to fly, as shown in this life group. This is probably done as a protection from animals. A small opening is left through which the male feeds the female and the young. The bird on the right is the black and blue fairy bluebird. On a branch in the upper left is a green bulbul.

111. The only species of parrot native to the eastern United States, the Carolina paroquet, is now extinct due to having been killed in great numbers by man. Although mainly inhabiting the southern areas, it was found as far north as Pennsylvania and the south shores of Lake Erie and Lake Michigan. The birds were considered destructive to fruit and grain.

112. The Greater Bird of Paradise is bowed forward, wings arched, the long plumes of the sides and flanks erected.

110

109

111

112

47

113. The red grouse with wings spread.

114. The long toes of the jaçana, a tropical American bird, permit it to walk on floating leaves, from which it eats snails and insects.

115. By cross breeding and selection for desired traits, man has produced strains different from the wild ancestral bird. The budgerigar is the ancestor of the budgies. The dove has descended from the wild rock dove.

116. The secretary bird, a long-legged African hawk, attacks and kills snakes by kicking them to death.

117. As many as 5,000 ants have been found in the stomach of one of these flickers.

118. Bird's eggs range in size from the tiny humming-bird egg to that of the extinct elephant bird. The size of the egg is usually directly related to the size of the bird. The woodcock (center) is typical of the size relationship. In species where the young are born naked and helpless, such as the meadow lark on the left, the egg is much smaller for the size of the bird. The kiwi lays the largest egg in proportion to its body size.

113

114

115

116

117

49

118

MAMMALS

120

STUDYING THE natural environment of the people of the United States has always been a primary concern of the Smithsonian Institution. Secretary Baird, as a young man before coming to the Institution, worked with Audubon collecting small mammals for his use in completing his *Quadrupeds of North America,* to be a companion to his great folio on American birds. He had also written the volumes on birds and mammals for the report on "Exploration and Surveys for a Railroad Route from the Mississippi to the Pacific Ocean," which naturalist Elliot Coues considered a greater and more widely felt influence than even Audubon's. Branching out from those of this continent to mammals of the world, the National Museum now exhibits one of the finest collections in the country.

121

122

Twenty-eight types, or orders, as they are called, of living mammals are known to have occurred, and eighteen of these still exist. Several of these orders are threatened with extinction. The eighteen orders living today are exemplified by the kangaroo, platypus, monkey, aardvark, mouse and squirrel, elephant, sloth, hyrax, bat, rabbit, manatee, horse, whale, pangolin, flying lemur, mole, and the two orders best known to the average person, the one comprising the camel, deer, and pig, and the other the dog and skunk. Many characteristics of mammals are discussed and illustrated with the actual animal, such as the beneficial free-tailed bat, which eats insects, the duckbilled platypus and the destructive woodchuck. The types and reasons for their habits, coloration and defenses are also covered. Full scale and minutely detailed settings give a beautiful and informative picture of many of the North American mammals.

119. The largest animal ever recorded in the modern world is the African elephant in the center of the Natural History Building that stands thirteen feet two inches high at the shoulder. A full twenty inches higher than Jumbo, the Ringling Brothers star elephant which was considered huge, the Smithsonian elephant weighed an estimated twelve tons while living. The skin alone weighed more than two tons when it was delivered to the Smithsonian taxidermists.

120. Several unrelated groups of tree-dwelling mammals have developed gliding membranes consisting

of a parachute-like fold of skin connecting their fore and hind limbs. These animals do not really fly, they merely leap and then glide from tree to tree. The bat is the only mammal capable of true flight.

121. The woodchuck of North America is particularly destructive of clover and alfalfa fields, consuming large amounts of forage. In addition, the earth from its burrows kills additional plants and makes harvesting difficult.

122. The duckbill platypus of Australia is one of the mammals known to use poison for offense or defense. There is no record of a human dying as a result of this poison.

123

124

123. The young of the rock wallaby are born alive and crawl unaided to the nipples of the mother's abdomen, where they remain until they have reached full development. Some marsupials, as this type is called, have abdominal pouches for protecting the undeveloped young.

124. The three types of mammals are characterized by the way they give birth and care for their young. The spiny anteater is an example of a monotreme, the only type of mammal whose young come from eggs. The young animals eat by lapping milk from the fur of a depressed area on the underside of the mother's body.

125. The placentals, of which the black-fronted duiker is one, are the most advanced of the mammals. The young are born alive and helpless although some of the hoofed animals such as the horse bear young which can move about with ease very soon after birth.

126. A Rocky Mountain puma or mountain lion rests near Yellowstone Falls. This member of the cat family is extremely adaptable, living in the mountains or the lowlands. The puma and the spotted jaguar are the only large cats in the New World.

127. One of the finest and most difficult taxidermy projects was the hippopotamus, the "river horse."

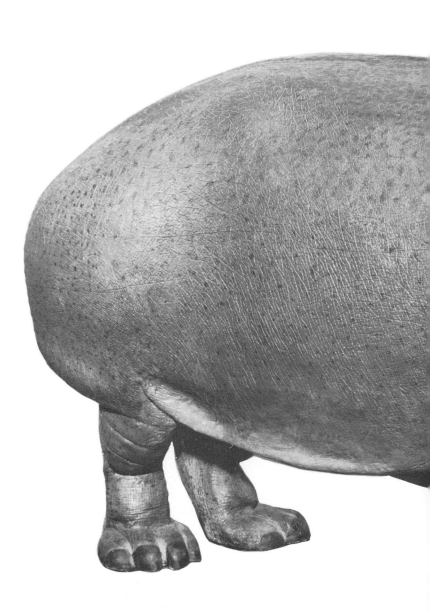

126

127

53

128. The dik-dik of eastern Africa is the smallest known antelope. The animals are unusual in that they apparently can go entirely without water except for that contained in the roots and bulbs they eat. The name is derived from the bird-like sound they make.

129 & 130. The lesser panda and the oryx have their eyes hidden in dark stripes of fur for protection.

131. The hartebeest or kongoni of East Africa, shown in this scene in Kenya, travels in small herds of from five to twenty. Much to the dismay of hunters, a self-appointed sentry of one or more of these animals stands on an anthill or boulder and watches for danger in the surrounding plain, giving the alarm to its own kind and to all other creatures besides. The small birds of the left are vitelline, or masked, weavers.

132. This pack of wolves is shown stalking a moose along the Colville River in Alaska. The largest may weigh 175 pounds. Near relatives of the dog, a pack usually consists of family groups of no more than eight or ten.

129

130

133

NORTH AMERICAN ARCHAEOLOGY

Hidden in the rocks that make up the North American continent are archaeological evidences of many prehistoric peoples. The land that now comprises forty-nine of the fifty states was inhabited by cultures of many types. The elaborate burial mounds of the Hopewell people of the Mississippi Valley, the stylized art forms in copper of the southeast, the ivory sculptures of the Aleutian Eskimos, indicate well established and advanced civilizations. Stone tools made by very early people predate the oldest remains of a human being in this hemisphere, the 10,000-or-more-year-old skull found at Midland, Texas (see fig. 133).

Because they have been found in so many parts of the country and have several distinct shapes, stone tools, probably spearheads, are the major clue to the earliest known peoples of North America. One type, called Folsom points after the place where they were first found, is a slender blade with a broad indentation down each side made by skillfully chipping a flake of stone. Because some of the spearheads were found near the bones of mammoths and extinct bison, these early hunters must have lived during the last great Ice Age. Study of the several shapes indicates that the east was populated by big game hunters, the west by food gatherers, and the northern areas by hunters and fishermen.

134. Folsom points.

135. The bison vertebra has a spear point embedded in it. The Folsom spearmen hunted a now extinct camel as well as bison. Charcoal from their campfires has been radiocarbon-dated as about 10,000 years old.

136. This chipped knife is from the Maine Red-paint culture, dated 1400 B.C. These people are known from their cemeteries in which large quantities of red ochre paint were found.

137. Some of the prehistoric foragers of the western plains were called dog-nomads. The bison supplied them with food, clothing, tools, shelter, and many items of everyday and ceremonial use. The hallmark of the foragers was the milling slab and handstone, used for grinding vegetables.

138. Agate Basin points of early big game hunters of the Black Hills have a distinctive laurel-leaf outline.

139. The purpose of these ceremonial carved shells is not certain but they seem to have been made to use as containers. An antlered and masked dancer with a bow is pictured on the shell at the top while a rattlesnake with antlers and four bodies appears on the one below. These shells are from eastern Oklahoma. Near the shells are diagrams showing the engravings.

140. The Old Copper Indians of the Upper Great Lakes region were the first metal workers in America, more than 5,000 years ago. The stone tools are from an ancient copper mine, found in Michigan. The harpoon heads, axheads, and crescent-shaped knives are of native copper.

141. Three water bottles show various types of pottery decoration. The one on the left is engraved, the middle one is sculptured with three human heads, and the one on the right is decorated with negative painting.

142. From the Central Valley of California comes this portable mortar for grinding seeds and nuts.

143. Cupstones were possibly used for cracking nuts by the archaic peoples of the Southeast.

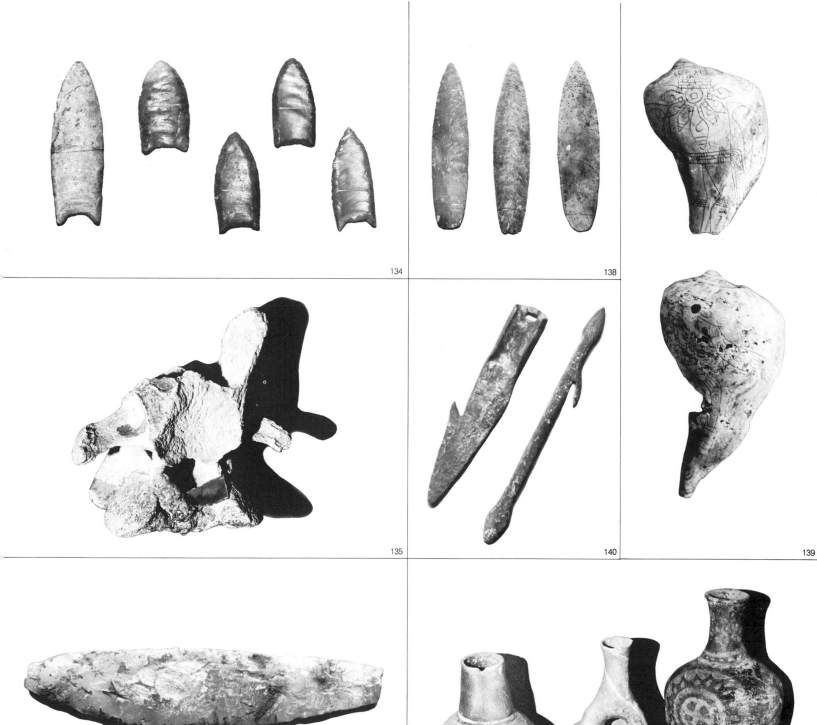

134

138

135

140

139

136

141

137

142

143

144. Wood carving reached a high level of refinement in south Florida during the fifteenth century. Because metal was unknown, the face was carved with sharpened shells and shark-tooth knives.

145. Many shell gorgets depicting human faces were found in graves and burial mounds. They may have been used as death masks.

146. Wood carvings such as this ceremonial mask from an Aleut burial cave were often deposited with the dead. Unalaska.

147. The mid-Atlantic peoples were influenced by the *death cult,* a dramatic religious movement that spread northward from the southeastern United States about 1500. This weeping-eye shell mask is identical in shape, size, and style to death cult objects from areas to the southwest.

148. Ceremonial mask from an Aleut burial cave. Lenoi Island.

144

145

146

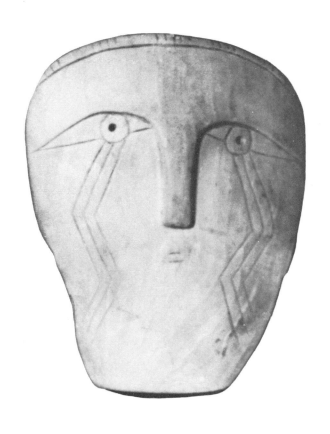

147

148

149

151

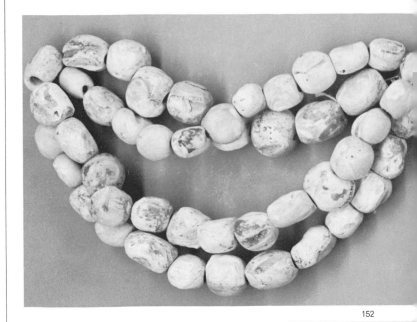

152

150

153

149. This head effigy vase from Arkansas is an example of prehistoric sculpture from the southeast United States.

150. Another prehistoric head effigy vase from Arkansas.

151. Possibly used for scraping green corn from the cob, this deer jaw was used by villagers of the Great Plains about 1150 to 1300.

152. Objects from the Spiro Mound in Oklahoma include these columella beads.

153. The Stone disk was made by the Hopewell people, builders of great earthworks. It is carved with the outline of a human hand and probably was for ceremonial use.

154. These stone images are from Tennessee grave and village sites.

154

61

155

SMITHSONIAN SPONSORED EXPEDITIONS

IN 1842, the United States Exploring Expedition returned from a round-the-world voyage of almost four years duration. The government-sponsored expedition of six ships under the command of Captain Charles Wilkes, USN, was to have a profound influence on the Smithsonian Institution.

The purpose of the expedition was primarily to investigate the commercial whaling industry, but Captain Wilkes and a staff that included some of the nation's leading naturalists, geologists, mineralogists, taxidermists, and a philologist, had collected large numbers of artifacts of the peoples of the Pacific, including Hawaii, now the fiftieth state. The collections were turned over to the National Institute and later transferred to the Smithsonian. Since that time, many other expeditions have gone out under the sponsorship of the Institution and continue even today.

Experience resulting from one such expedition proved invaluable to Secretary of State William H. Seward at the time when Congress was sharply divided on whether or not to spend the great sum of money needed to buy Alaska from the Russians.

A naturalist, Robert Kennicott, who had studied under Baird, was put in charge of the scientists acompanying an expedition to Alaska for the Western Union Telegraph Company, which was considering the overland route for a telegraph line connecting the United States and Europe. After the party had reached Alaska, the project was dropped because of the success of the trans-Atlantic cable, but the expedition had explored much territory never before seen by white men.

Kennicott died suddenly in Alaska but one of the party, H. M. Bannister, upon his return to Washington, joined Baird in advising Seward of the riches in fish, timber, furs, copper, and gold to be found there. Thus was the Secretary of State able to justify the immense expenditure of money for an unknown land.

Artifacts from many sources, including expeditions, comprise the comprehensive coverage of the life of the peoples of the Pacific Islands.

Another famous expedition under the direction of the Smithsonian began when ten men in four boats started down the Green and Colorado Rivers, the first white men to traverse the Grand Canyon. This impressive achievement, under the command of John Wesley Powell who had lost his right arm at Shiloh in the Civil War, was to lead to the establishment of the Bureau of American Ethnology. The bureau was made a part of the Smithsonian Institution with Powell as its director, a position he held until his death in 1902.

The bureau has studied the evidence of aboriginal peoples throughout the western hemisphere and has published many works dealing with these cultures. At a time when the American Indian was considered by most people as a dangerous savage to be done away with, the bureau was recording their languages and songs, preserving their arts, and documenting their cultures. By law, it is required to turn over to the National Museum all archaeological and ethnological collections when it is finished with them, thus contributing much to the present-day exhibition halls covering these subjects.

155. Wooden image from the Fiji Islands, United States Exploring Expedition, 1838—1842.

NORTH AMERICAN INDIANS

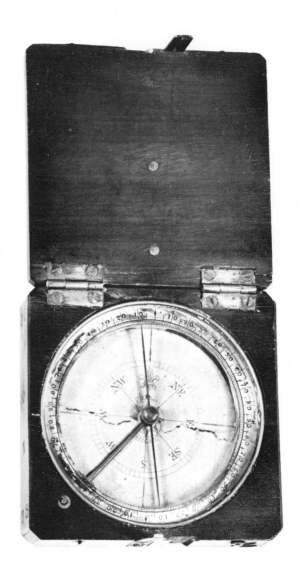

156

Tʜᴏᴍᴀs Jᴇꜰꜰᴇʀsᴏɴ, when he signed the Louisiana Purchase, realized that almost nothing was known about the newly acquired land that had doubled the size of the United States. Information of the kind needed could only be obtained by sending forth an exploration party. Thus was born the Lewis and Clark Expedition that, with the Sibly Expedition to the Red River in 1803, was the first great scientific exploration.

Lewis and Clark, on their travels through the northwest country, collected many examples of unfamiliar plants and animals. Two plants they discovered, the *Lewisia* and the *Clarkia,* were named for them. They also brought back artifacts of unknown Indian tribes.

The transfer of the Bureau of American Ethnology to the Smithsonian set the Institution on a path of study of the American Indian which it continues to pursue today. The bureau's collections of ceremonial and everyday objects of Indian life have come to the Department of Ethnology of the United States National Museum, which has prepared exhibitions of life-size Indian groups and contains comprehensive study collections of North American anthropology, archaeology, and ethnology.

One of the bureau's most valuable contributions to a knowledge of the aboriginal American was the study of the cultures, and the collection of artifacts, of many fast-disappearing Indian tribes. The Hall of Native Peoples of the Americas incorporates many of these fascinating objects that might have been lost forever.

157

156. Compass and case carried by Lewis and Clark on their expedition to the Northwest.

157. Natural forces and the vagaries of nature have always demanded great inventiveness from mankind, but the manner and skill with which the Polar Eskimos meet the extreme cold and sparse food supply of the Arctic region are particularly admirable. The way these northernmost people of the world make some of the extreme conditions of their environment work for them, instead of against them, is graphically demonstrated in the various exhibits.

Eskimo clothing must be warm but light in weight. A man's winter outfit of caribou skins (third from left) from northwestern Canada is strong, warm, and very light because of air-filled cavities in each hair of the fur. The entire outfit is warmer than woolen clothing twice its weight.

Sealskins make up this Labrador Eskimo man's spring

158

suit (left) that is strong and waterproof but not warm enough for winter use.

Second from left is an Alaskan woman's costume of ground squirrel skins which is warm, flexible but fairly fragile.

On the far right is an Alaskan summer parka of eider-duck skins which is warm and very light, but far too fragile for general wear.

158. Stone headed war club and handle of rawhide from the Northwest Plains Indians. Collected by Lewis and Clark in 1805 and 1806.

65

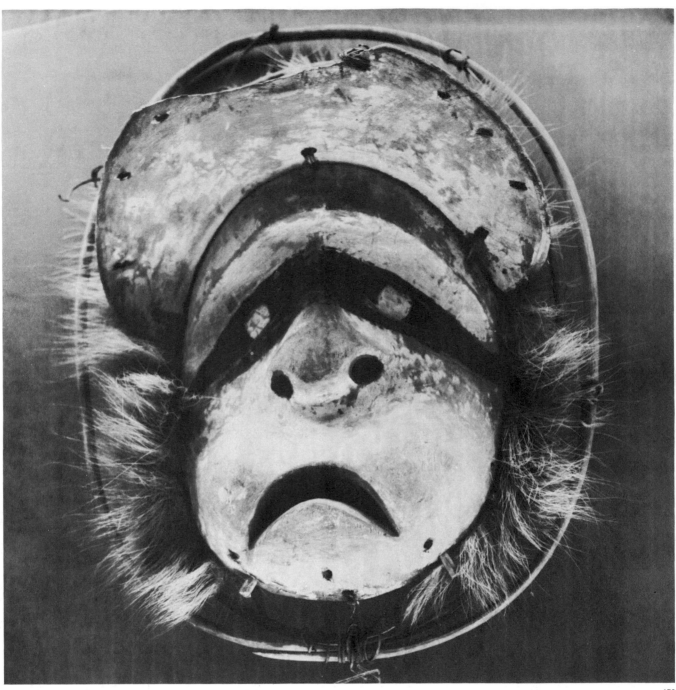

159

159. This Eskimo ceremonial mask was worn at festivals when the Eskimos gave thanks to the spirits for bringing them luck in hunting and fishing.

160. Iroquois men of the False Face Society wear such masks as these and go from house to house casting out evil spirits that cause sickness. Each mask represents a spirit endowed by the creator of the world with the power to cure disease.

161. The Seminoles inhabited the Florida everglades. A typical man's costume often combined trade cloth such as calico with native materials such as the feathers of local birds, and leggings of native deerskin.

162. Outside the tipi entrance a hard-working young woman crushes cherries with their pits for use in making pemmican, an Indian delicacy made of the fruit and sun-dried buffalo meat. Her recipe is on view for modern cooks who may wish to try it.

160

161

162

An Indian Recipe: PEMMICAN

Sun-dried buffalo meat, sliced thin; Buffalo fat; Marrow grease; Dried unpitted wild cherries (optional)

Pulverize meat in rawhide mortar with stone pestle. Melt fat and grease and stir in to taste. Crush cherries with pits; add as desired. Pack in hide sacks. Store until winter.

Calories: 3500 per lb.   Average serving: 3/4 lb. per day

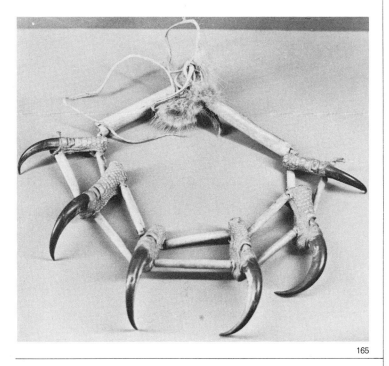

165

166

163. The life of the Plains Indians revolved around
the buffalo, or bison, as it is more correctly named. Nearly
one hundred objects of daily and ceremonial use are
fashioned from parts of this animal. Indian homes of buffalo
skin were designed to be packed on horseback.

This tipi, which was exhibited at the Philadelphia
Centennial in 1876, was the year-round home of an average
Arapaho family. It is covered with fourteen buffalo skins
sewn with sinew thread and ornamented with porcupine
quillwork. The skins weigh one hundred pounds and are
supported by sixteen pine foundation poles with a total
weight of 256 pounds. Two other poles support the adjustable
flaps above the smoke hole. Two horses were needed
to transport the tipi from one campsite to another.

The shield and weapons of the owner hang on a tripod
outside the doorway. Inside, the host sits opposite
the doorway with male guests on the left while the wife
and female guests sit to the right. It is impolite to pass
between the host and the central fire.

164. Before they had horses the Blackfoot Indians could
round up a herd of buffalo. Agile young men disguised
in buffalo skins lured the herd to the edge of a cliff, where
the leader's momentum carried it to its death below,
the rest of the herd following. A corral at the base
of the cliff prevented the escape of any survivors.

165. A man's necklace of eagle claws and bones. Plains Indians.

166. This tall cedar totem pole marked the entrance
to a Haida Indian home. The doorway is at the bottom
and is thirty-three inches high. The family crests
of the owners are the grizzly bear and the killer whale.
The two figures at the top are called the watchmen.

69

167. The Chilkat women of the Tlingit tribe were skilled weavers. The woman at the loom is holding some of the long warp strands which have a core of cedar-bark twine and have their lower ends tied in bladder bags to keep them clean. The white areas of the pattern are made with undyed mountain goat wool such as is in the wooden box behind the weaver. The black is obtained by dyeing the wool in a solution of urine and hemlock bark. Blue is from copper and yellow from a lichen. A half year was often required for the weaving of a blanket, each weft strand being inserted by hand. The men painted the pattern boards (right) to guide the weavers.

The Salish women spun yarn sheared from their small woolly dogs and wove blankets from the wool. They also made belts and pack straps (upper right) from the skins of these dogs.

168

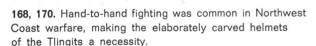

167

168, 170. Hand-to-hand fighting was common in Northwest Coast warfare, making the elaborately carved helmets of the Tlingits a necessity.

169. The fireplace is the kind found in Hopi Indian homes. The unmarried girls wear their hair in whorls at the side of their heads while the married woman wears her hair down and braided. The girls on the left are making corn meal by crushing parched kernels of corn between stones. The corn is being toasted or parched in the large pot on the fire. The woman is making wafer bread by spreading the batter thinly on a flat stone griddle. It cooks quickly and is peeled off and folded.

On the right is a young rabbit hunter with his carved wood throwing stick. The man is bringing in corn just harvested in wicker baskets. The girl in the front is weaving a basket.

171. The desert people wore little clothing. The Seri man at the left wears a loin covering of pelican skins. The Mohave man wears a breechcloth of cottonwood or willow bark. The sandals are for traveling. The pair made of rawhide on the left are Pima and the Mohave pair on the right are of bark.

172. Carved wooden feast bowl, about four feet long, represents Tsonoquoa, a female cannibal who was killed by the hero of a Kwakiutl legend. In the bowl is a wooden dipper.

170

169

171

172

THE PACIFIC

173

EVER SINCE the members of the United States Exploring Expedition of 1838 brought back many strange and exotic objects from the unknown islands of the far Pacific, Americans have been eager to learn about the remote corners of the world. Whalers and clipper ships returned with evidence of tropical paradises and oriental lands, causing the mingling of austere New England household goods and furniture with Chinese vases and Polynesian woodcarvings.

The Department of Ethnology, through its exhibits in the United States National Museum, has always tried to illustrate the habits and cultures of these people so that they can be better appreciated and understood by everyone. Over the years the collections have grown so that now the material exhibited tells a comprehensive story of the faraway peoples of the world.

173. Wearing a red stone "hat" quarried from a volcano crater, this monumental stone statue was erected as a memorial to the dead, whose spirits were believed to enter living persons. This Easter Island statue is about twelve feet high.

174. Shown is a painting on bark of the lightning-being who lives in a waterhole. The bands between the hands and feet represent lightning.

175. The segment of a flat carving was done by the Maoris.

175

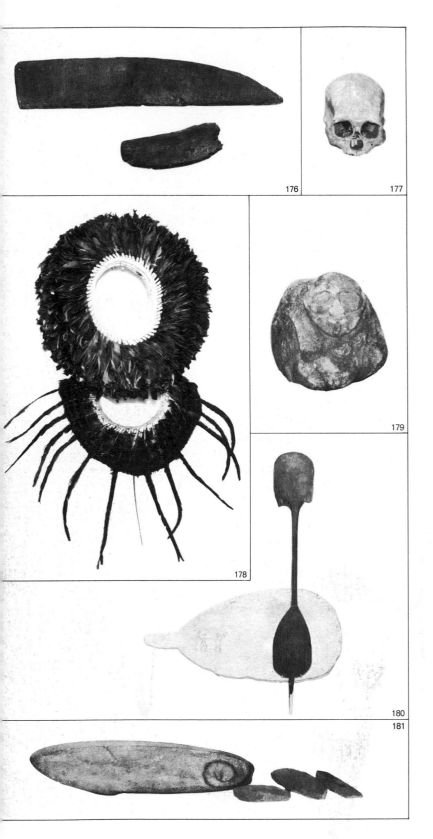

THE EASTERN South Sea Islands, known as Polynesia (including Hawaii, New Zealand, Samoa and Easter Island) are not nationally unified but are inhabited by people of similar cultural characteristics. Easter Island culture is unique in Polynesia, so strange that many theories have been presented concerning the origin of these strange people but scientists have now proved that natives, language and culture are clearly native to Polynesia.

176. The origin and meaning of the unique mnemonic tablets are shrouded in mystery and no known native now living can read them. Twenty-one tablets exist, all in museums.

177. The human skull is engraved with the "proper" design to increase the fertility of men and animals.

178. Headdresses of chicken feathers had symbolic and spiritual meaning when worn in war, ceremonies, or dancing.

179. A unique tiki whose use is unknown but which resembles in size and shape boundary stones found on other Polynesian islands.

180. Shown is an Easter Island dance wand and carved ceremonial paddle.

181. The spiral carving on the end of the stone ceremonial adze is unique. The adze was probably for ceremonial use.

182. Wooden ancestral figures are of deified ancestors and spirits of the dead. They were usually wrapped in bark cloth and worn around the necks of the descendants. The figure on the right is from the 1850 Cook Expedition.

183. New Guinea wood carvings include, top left, a canoe ornament, a mask to the right, the large spirit figure, and to the right of it, a food hanger. At the bottom is a ceremonial drum. Other objects include masks, and at the far right, a trophy skull hanger and an ancestral tablet.

182

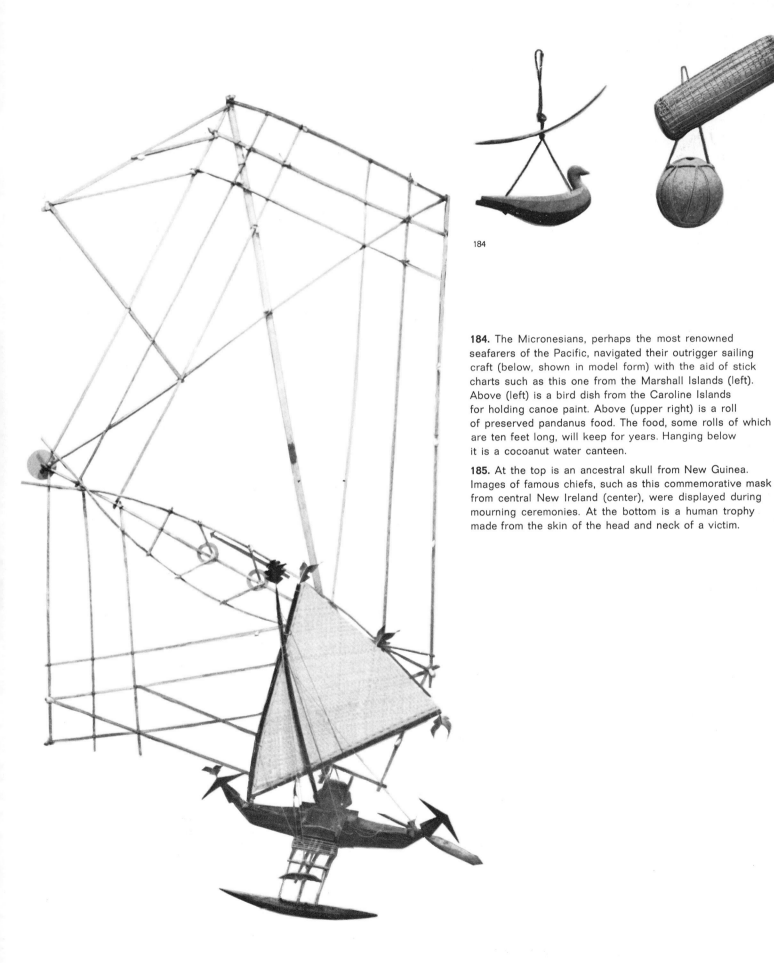

184. The Micronesians, perhaps the most renowned seafarers of the Pacific, navigated their outrigger sailing craft (below, shown in model form) with the aid of stick charts such as this one from the Marshall Islands (left). Above (left) is a bird dish from the Caroline Islands for holding canoe paint. Above (upper right) is a roll of preserved pandanus food. The food, some rolls of which are ten feet long, will keep for years. Hanging below it is a cocoanut water canteen.

185. At the top is an ancestral skull from New Guinea. Images of famous chiefs, such as this commemorative mask from central New Ireland (center), were displayed during mourning ceremonies. At the bottom is a human trophy made from the skin of the head and neck of a victim.

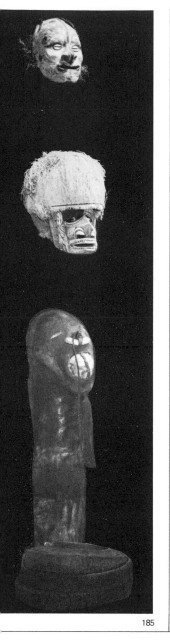

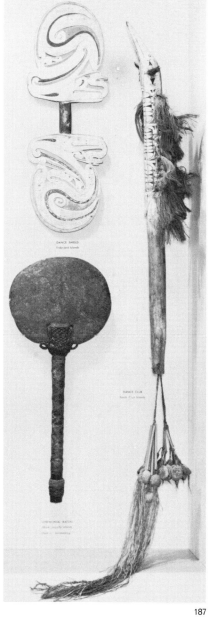

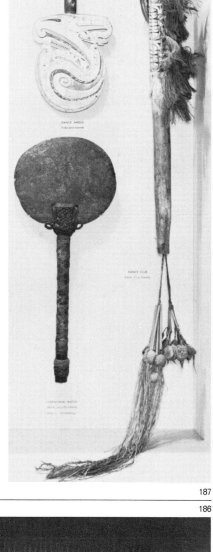

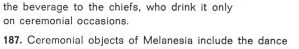

188

186. A Samoan village's highest ranking maiden and her attendants, shown in this group of life-size figures, pound kava roots and mix them with water. The young men carry the beverage to the chiefs, who drink it only on ceremonial occasions.

187. Ceremonial objects of Melanesia include the dance shield of the Trobriand Islands, top left; beneath it a ceremonial baton from the Loyalty Islands; and at the right, a Santa Cruz Island dance club.

188. A Maori feather box which was suspended overhead to protect its valuable contents.

189. Below are an Austral Island ceremonial paddle, a Maori sparring club, and a Tonga war club.

189

190

ASIA

AMERICA WAS discovered because Columbus was searching for a direct sea route to the Far East. For centuries the Western World has looked to the Orient for spices, silks, and exotic goods but has made little effort to learn of the people who produce them. A journey to those far-off lands now takes as many hours as it used to take months. The peoples of Asia are getting closer, and the exhibit in the Hall of Asian Cultures does much to bridge the gap that remains.

190. Chinese character "tiger" written here by Beue Tann (Tan Peh-yu) is the emblem of civil authority and military courage and is often used to ward off misfortune.

191. Representing the Great Physician, this iron Korean Buddha from Wonju holds a container of medicine. From the Koryo Dynasty, 918 to 1392.

192. Lord Shiva, the Hindu god of destruction and regeneration, is shown with his consort, Parvati, the divine mother and goddess of terror. She is worshipped more than any other female Hindu deity. These statues, made recently in Madras, use centuries-old metalworking techniques and artistic treatment.

193. Hindu temples of India and Pakistan were built for the god and the pilgrim, not to shelter a congregation. The perforated inserts of this temple window of the Dravidian style, probably late eighteenth century, admit light and air but maintain privacy. The great temple at Madura, with its pylon-like towers, was built in 1560 in this style.

194. The dignity and burden-bearing potential of the elephant have given it architectural significance both as a base and for decorative elements.

195. With arms that are hinged, the ornate and richly decorated puppets of Malaya enact roles in popular Hindu drama in a specially constructed theater. A "master of puppets" manipulates the figures and speaks for them. The puppets' shadows, which the audience sees cast on a thin muslin curtain, are not just silhouettes but, due to perforated designs cut into the puppet shapes, are filled with elaborate patterns and textures.

193

194

195

196

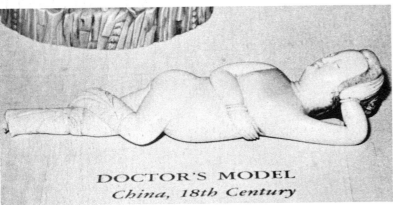

DOCTOR'S MODEL
China, 18th Century

197

198

196. The cow and calf are carved from wood and painted. The cow is sacred to all Hindu sects and personifies all the gods.

197. Women patients were not examined directly by their doctors but would indicate their symptoms on an ivory doctor's model such as this eighteenth century one from China.

198. Painted in oils on the back of glass, this painting from Iran shows French influence of about 1840.

199. Typical of Japanese folk crafts is this Oita covered pot used for storing water. It has a chatter mark design.

200. An example of the first Buddhist art style in China, the statue of a Buddhist divinity is of the Northern Wei Period, probably A.D. 531.

ARTS AND INDUSTRIES

201. Power for all the machinery of the Centennial Exhibition in Philadelphia in 1876 was supplied by this Corliss Engine. A model is on display in the Smithsonian exhibit on power.

THE FIRST American World's Fair or its equivalent was the Philadelphia Centennial Exhibition of 1876, which celebrated the one hundredth anniversary of the signing of the Declaration of Independence. Spencer Fullerton Baird was one of the Board appointed by President Grant to direct the government's activities and exhibits. Professor Baird was particularly concerned with the Smithsonian and Fish Commission's exhibit which was prepared with the help of George Brown Goode, a new staff member who was later to become an important force in shaping the destiny of the Institution.

The Centennial proved that the Machine Age was in full flower when President Grant and the Emperor of Brazil started the four thousand horsepower Corliss steam engine in the Machine Hall which supplied power to the machinery of the Exposition.

When the fair closed on November 10, the disposition of the many exhibits, Federal and State as well as those of many foreign countries, became a problem. Secretary Henry reported that of the forty or so countries and governments represented, thirty-four had presented their choicest exhibits to the Smithsonian for the National Museum. Nevada, Montana, and Utah presented their complete mineral exhibits. Professor Baird was responsible for suggesting that the Smithsonian was the logical place for exhibits covering such diverse subjects.

The problem was what to do with this tremendous amount of valuable material. The Smithsonian building was overflowing and additional exhibit space was needed. It was three years before Congress appropriated the money. Baird had succeeded Henry as secretary and the new building was one of the major problems he faced.

The solution decided upon was a "temporary" building of two and one half acres, erected just east of the Smithsonian building and built so cheaply that the structure is noted for being the cheapest building ever erected by the government in Washington. In fact, unspent money was returned to the Treasury, something unheard of before or since.

The building, first known as the National Museum but later called Arts and Industries, was first used as the scene of President Garfield's Inaugural Ball before the museum exhibits were installed. The brick building with its high ceiling and arched exhibit halls contained the Smithsonian's vast collection of historical memorabilia and technological specimens from 1881 until January, 1964, when the new museum building was opened. Airplanes of the Smithsonian's collection still fly from the high ceilings of this eighty-year-old "temporary" structure that for many decades was the Smithsonian Institution in the minds of most Americans.

If they were to be exhibited or safely preserved, the exhibits that came to the Smithsonian from the Centennial required a space estimated to be four times as large as the original building. The report to Congress dated February 25, 1878, described them as "coals, marbles, and other ornamental minerals and varied products of the aboriginal races of North America" which would supplement the exhibits already on display. In addition, there were technical exhibits which would make the United States National Museum "one of the great industrial and economical displays of the natural resources of the globe."

Secretary Baird, in his 1879 report, said, "... The new building will be devoted more particularly to industrial exhibits, intended to show the animal and mineral resources of the United States and their practical applications to the wants or luxuries of man. The department of anthropology will also be largely represented. How far natural history can find a place in the building will depend upon the space required for the collections mentioned. It is confidently expected that this building when finished will be one of the most attractive objects of the kind extant and but little inferior to the celebrated museums of foreign countries...."

The new building cost about six cents per cubic foot of space.

Electricity first gleamed forth from the Smithsonian when in 1881 the Brush Electrical Company presented the museum with "storage cells and a dynamo suitable for operating between thirty and forty incandescent and 16-candle power lamps in the lecture hall." In 1895 a gas engine and dynamo were installed in the basement of the south tower of the main building, but it was 1902 before a fairly complete electrical system was installed by employees of the museum. Electric burglar alarms also were installed as were telephones.

The impact of the Philadelphia Centennial on the National Museum is most obvious when the departments comprising the Museum in 1875 are compared with the organization of ten years later. In 1875 the departments, then called divisions, of Mineralogy, Ornithology, Conchology, and Ethnology (including Indian materials and archaeology) are listed. In 1886 Ethnology was part of the Department of Anthropology which also included Aboriginal American Pottery, Archaeology, and Arts and Industries. This last section contained collections of Materia Medica, Textile Industries, Fisheries and Animal Products, Foods, Historical Relics, Paints and Dyes, Physical Apparatus, Oils and Gums, Chemical Products, Musical Instruments, Modern Instruments, and the Catlin Gallery. It is likely that all these collections except the Catlin Gallery and the Physical Apparatus came from the 1876 Centennial. In 1885 the Section of Transportation was organized.

As written in the Smithsonian Annual Report of 1912, "The Centennial Exhibition of 1876 afforded the first opportunity for establishing a department of the industrial arts on a creditable basis."

CATLIN GALLERY

GEORGE CATLIN as a boy in Wilkes-Barre, Pennsylvania, dreamed of the Wild West and Indians. His mother had been captured as a young girl by Indians in the Wyoming Massacre and her stories had stirred his imagination to such an extent that he gave up his career in law to go west and paint the American Indian. His canvases, painted from life while traveling with General William Clark (of the Lewis and Clark Expedition) up the Mississippi and Missouri Rivers, and in the Kansas and Oklahoma Territories, are a unique record of the Sioux, Cheyenne, Comanche, Omaha, Mandan, Kickapoo, and other tribes of the Great Plains Woodlands and the Far Northwest.

He painted many landscapes while traveling two thousand miles to the mouth of the Yellowstone River on board the *Yellowstone*, the first steamboat to sail up the Missouri River. He produced over six hundred paintings, most of them portraits of Indian chiefs, braves, and squaws, but which included scenes of hunting, and village life and customs.

From 1833 to 1852 he exhibited about five hundred of his Indian paintings in New York, Philadelphia, Washington, Boston, London, and Paris.

Seven years after his death in 1872, his paintings, partially damaged by fire, were presented to the Smithsonian Institution, and the Catlin Gallery became one of the important exhibitions on view in the new Arts and Industries Building. In the years since, his paintings have become increasingly important in the study of the aboriginal American.

202

202. View in "Cross Timbers," Texas.

203. *Four Bears,* Mandan chief.

204. *Rabbit's Skin Leggings,* one of two Nez Percé Indians who had visited in 1834. Catlin painted them in Sioux costumes on their return journey up the Missouri River.

205. *She Who Bathes Her Knees,* wife of *High Wolf,* a Cheyenne tribal chief.

206. Wife of *Keokuk.*

MERCHANT MARINE

ARCHAEOLOGICAL EVIDENCE points toward the Vikings as being the first people of the Old World to reach the New. Then, centuries later, came the great discoverers, Columbus, Hudson, John Cabot, Balboa, and Cartier, who in their search for a passage to the Orient, led the way for the great migration from the old traditions of Europe to an uncharted way of life across the sea.

The sea was a source of food, power, transportation, and communication and was the link with the homeland for the early colonists. The ships they used to cross the Atlantic, to fish the great fishing banks off New England, and soon to trade with the most distant corners of the globe, established a firm foundation for American colonial life and were the basis of much of the economic greatness of the nation today.

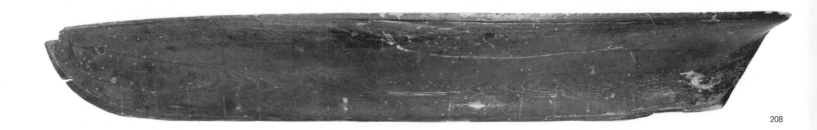

207. This model of a ninth century Viking ship was based on a Gokstad ship excavated in Norway in 1880. The original vessel was 79 feet long and had a 16½ foot beam.

208. This builder's block model of the privateer *Snap Dragon* was made before 1812 and is the oldest half-model in the collection.

209. The 177-foot-long whaling schooner *Orca* was built in San Francisco in 1882. It was abandoned off Point Barrow, Alaska, in 1889.

210. The *Francis Skiddy*, a Hudson River steamer of 1848. traveled twenty-three or twenty-four miles an hour.

211. The fishing schooner *Mary Fernald* (above) was built in 1875 at Gloucester, Massachusetts. Built for transatlantic service, the *Mauretania* (below) was the sister ship of the *Lusitania*.

212. The Chesapeake Bay skipjack or "crabscraper," the *Jess Willard*, was built in 1915 in Maryland.

213. The *Fredonia* of 1889 influenced the design of New England fishing schooners for fifteen years.

214. The square-sterned Chebacco boat was used for fishing.

214

EVERYDAY LIFE IN AMERICA

URING THE early years when the Smithsonian's museum collections were forming, early American housewares and furniture, if collected at all, were considered as heirlooms or as beautiful or useful objects for use. But it is doubtful if they were ever considered suitable for exhibiting in a museum. Useful products came to the institution, along with many other items, from the 1876 Philadelphia Exposition but were thought of as examples of American industrial strength and output. Then, in 1897, John Brenton Copp of Stonington, Connecticut, gave to the Smithsonian the famous collection of Copp family belongings that had been exhibited at the World's Columbian Exposition in Chicago in 1893. Thus commonplace tools and utensils as well as masterpieces of silver and cabinet work began to be preserved as historical examples through which the cultural development of the nation could be traced.

Now, enriched by many other gifts and numbering fifteen thousand or more items, the collection contains many objects that are works of art in their own right but are exhibited for the important role they played in the everyday history of America.

215

216. Jonathan Copp settled in Stonington, Connecticut, early in the eighteenth century. Those of his descendants who remained in Stonington carefully preserved the family belongings of the eighteenth and early nineteenth centuries. The framed silhouettes are of John Brown Copp, top, Samuel Copp, and Mary Copp.

216

W HEN THE early colonists sailed for North America, they had heard tales of savage Indians and the forbidding wilderness that lay ahead of them. They brought little with them but the many crafts and skills that they had learned in their native lands. They found a land rich in natural resources which they learned how to use from the Indians or through their own ingenuity. Over the years the English, Dutch, German, French, and Spanish settlers modified their traditions to meet the unfamiliar conditions they found, and created a new and vital civilization that had its basis in Europe but was distinctly American.

217

218

220

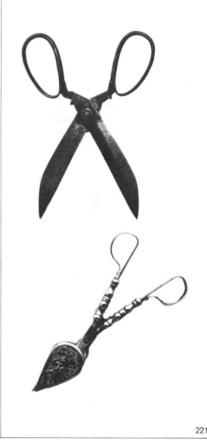

221

219

215. Weathervanes were often masterpieces of the tinsmith's art. The nineteenth century tin weathercock was made for a parish church in Quebec but was never used.

217. The seventeenth century brass curfew was used for covering coals in the fireplace at night.

218. The Dutch and Flemish have always been noted for their tile work. The four tiles shown are Dutch majolica of the mid-seventeenth century.

219. The pewter tankard on the left is from Switzerland and is dated 1754. In the center is a Swiss eighteenth century pewter wine can. On the right is a copper wine measure from the Austrian Tyrol.

220. The carved chest of about 1700 from Norway was originally not painted.

221. The brass candle snuffers at the bottom are French, late sixteenth century. Above are wrought-iron scissors.

222

223

94

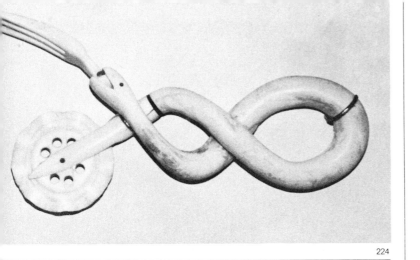

224

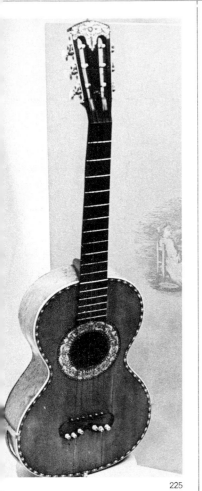

225

226

227

228

222. Carved from redwood around 1850, this figure
was used as a gun shop sign in San José, California.

223. The influence of Spanish art, architecture, and decorative
design still extant in many parts of the New World
is shown in this wood sculpture, carved and painted
by Captain Bernardo Miera y Pacheco for a Zuni Mission
church in New Mexico.

224. This Colonial pie crimper, which is about six inches
long, was used to mark the edges of pies and tarts.

225. The Spanish guitar dates from the seventeenth
or early eighteenth century.

226. Typical of the formal architecture of eighteenth
century America is this ornamental finial from the steeple
of Christ Church (Old North Church), Boston, built in 1740.
The lanterns which signaled to Paul Revere on his famous
ride were hung from the belfry just below this finial.

227. The French in North America used utilitarian cupboards
such as this late eighteenth century armoire from Quebec.

228. Fire protection was one of the domestic duties
of a farmer. Each fire fighter brought his own bucket, such
as the one shown, which was used by a volunteer fire
company in the early nineteenth century.

229. Most Colonial children played with homemade dolls. In well-to-do homes there were elegant dolls imported from France and Germany. On the left are French wax costume dolls of the early eighteenth century. In the center are bisque porcelain dolls and the peddler doll of the nineteenth century. In the oval on the right is an Italian wax crèche doll.

230. Alcoholic beverages were widely used in the Colonies. In the seventeenth century beer and cider were often made at home and were drunk with all meals. Wines were imported. The wine bottles are early eighteenth century.

231. Shown is a panel parlor from the Ruben Bliss House, Springfield, Massachusetts, dated 1754. A joiner by trade, Bliss bought an old house in 1753 and "modernized" it by installing Georgian style paneling and classical pilasters.

232. This parlor was one of the two rooms on the ground floor of William Eley's house, Isle of Wight County, Virginia. The elaborate woodwork shows a successful imitation of the architectural interiors of the great Virginia plantations. The date is about 1770.

233. New England furnishings of the early eighteenth century included locally made furniture that had become lighter and more elegant than that of the earlier century. The "bofat" or corner cupboard had just been introduced, giving a touch of classical formality. The translucent "bull's eye" panes in the window were used where a view was not needed.

232

233

97

234. Silver design of the Federal period was greatly influenced by classical forms found in Pompeii and Herculaneum. Shown are many superb examples of eighteenth century American silverwork.

235. Many of the household objects were fashioned by the Colonists from materials easily available. The soapstone potato baker is beautifully proportioned. The illustration shows how the "bow-drill" drink mixer was used.

235

237

238

236. The combination ice-cream parlor, candy shop and bakery was a turn-of-the-century institution in most cities. Stohlman's Confectionery Shop in Georgetown was a typical example. Operated by J. William Stohlman until 1957, it was patronized regularly by genteel Washington, D.C., families. The original cases, paneling, tables, chairs, candy molds and cartons are shown in a display based on a photograph taken about 1900.

237. Since Colonial times advertising has expressed the American capacity for exuberance and exaggeration. During the nineteenth century it was particularly colorful,

uninhibited, and often naive. On the left is a late nineteenth century cigar-store Indian. As early as the seventeenth century in England, the American Indian was the traditional tobacconist.

238. The drawer cabinet was used by an artist for storing paints. It is signed "Thomas Barnet."

239. Shown being installed in the Museum of History and Technology is a miller's log house of about 1740 from Delaware.

240. This ceramic colander was used in colonial America.

239

240

TEXTILES

HEN SAMUEL SLATER built from memory the first successful cotton spinning machines in this country, he started one of the earliest American industries and changed the New England countryside from a land of farmers and craftsmen to the major industrial area of North America.

The history of textiles is almost as old as the history of man himself. Clothing, along with food and shelter, is one of the basic needs of human beings. Fabrics formed by knitting threads together date from prehistoric times. The ancient Egyptians wove linen cloth, and weaver's tools have been found in early Peruvian graves.

The American colonists raised, spun, and wove almost all their own textiles, with only the wealthy able to import silks and brocades from Europe. Yankee ingenuity was soon put to work to improve old methods and invent new machines to speed up and simplify the making of textiles, climaxing in the new glass and synthetic fabrics of the twentieth century.

241. The process of preparing the raw fibers was slow and laborious. Yarn was spun by hand on the traditional spinning wheel. The larger wheel is a late eighteenth century wool wheel owned by Louisa Wells of Loudon, New Hampshire, whose birth date is marked on the end of the cross support.

242. All young girls learned to do many kinds of needlework. The sampler by Elizabeth Taylor was made in 1758 to demonstrate her skill with many kinds of decorative stitches.

EXOD

God speaks these words and said. i am The
Lord Thy God

I

Thou shalt have none other Gods but me

II

Thou shalt not make To Thy self any gra
ven image nor The Likeness of any

III

Thou shalt not Take The Name of The Lord
Thy God in vain for The Lord will not hold
him Guiltless That Taketh his Name in vain

IV

remember That Thou keep holy The sabba
th day six days shalt Thou Labour and do
all That Thou hast To do but The seventh
day is The sabbath of The Lord Thy God in

Chap XX

V

honour Thy father and Thy mother
That Thy days may be long in The land
which The Lord thy God giveth thee

VI

Thou shalt do no murder

VII

Thou shalt Not Commit adultery

VIII

Thou shalt not steal

IX

Thou shalt not bear false witness against
Thy neighbour X

Thou shalt not Covet Thy neighbours
house Thou shalt not covet Thy neighbo
urs wife nor his servant nor his maid nor
his ox nor his ass nor any thing that is his

Elizabeth Taylor mark This sampler in The II year of her age

17   58

242

101

243

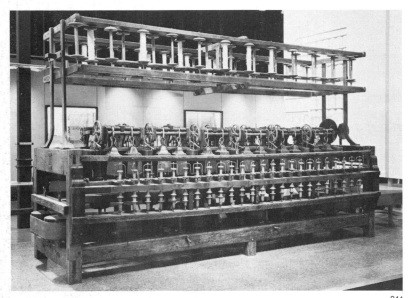

244

245

246

243. Hargrave's spinning jenny was the first machine for spinning cotton. The model was made from the English inventor's patent specifications of 1770. Centuries-old textile hand processing began to give way to mechanization.

244. Before coming to America in 1789 Samuel Slater had served as an apprentice in Jedediah Strutt's cotton mills in England. Working entirely from memory, he supervised the building of the first successful cotton spinning machinery in this country at Providence, Rhode Island. Shown is Slater's spinning frame dated 1790.

245. This carding machine was made by Slater in 1790 and was in use for more than thirty years.

246. Samuel Slater (engraving).

247. Shown is an 1806 French toile.

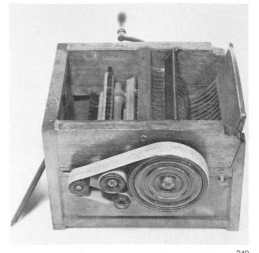

249

248. Used in Maine in the late eighteenth and early nineteenth centuries, this hand-and-foot-powered loom was used to weave the everyday fabrics of the time such as linsey-woolsey, which had a natural linen warp and an indigo-blue weft.

248

249. The ginning of cotton, or the removal of the cotton seeds from the fibers in preparation for spinning yarn, was perhaps more of a chore than the spinning itself. In 1794 Eli Whitney's invention for separating fibers from seeds revolutionized the textile industry and made cotton an economical crop for the southern states. The inventor himself made this model of his cotton gin around 1800.

250. Each appliquéd square of this autographed presentation quilt represents the work of one of the ladies of the Presbyterian Church, Maltaville, New York, and bears her autograph. The quilt, shown in its entirety, was presented in 1847 to the wife of the pastor.

251. The automatic bobbin changer on this 1895 Northrop loom was invented by John Northrop in 1891. The empty bobbin is automatically ejected and replaced by a filled bobbin.

252. Woven in the United States, this Jacquard double woven coverlet has a bird and flower design and a bird-in-tree border.

252

253

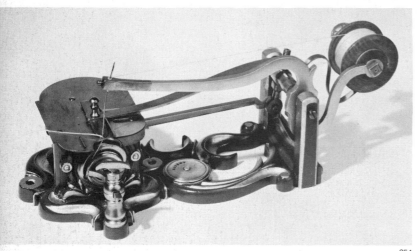

254

255

256

253. Native embroiderers of the Philippines presented this handkerchief of cotton embroidery on piña (pineapple fiber) cloth to Mrs. Theodore Roosevelt.

Made in Paraguay, this Nanduti lace handkerchief on the right uses the characteristic wheel motif.

254. This stationary bobbin patent model is dated 1852.

255. Shown is A. F. Johnson's 1857 sewing machine.

256. Many inventors attempted to devise a practical sewing machine. By the middle of the nineteenth century it became obvious that no one person could produce a successful sewing machine without infringing on the patented processes of others. The result was the pooling of the patents of several holders and the forming of a trust, the Sewing Machine Combination. Included were Elias Howe, Grover and Baker, the Singer Company, and Wheeler and Wilson. Any manufacturer using their patents paid the combination a royalty of $15.00 per machine. Shown are patent models of some early sewing machines. This is the original model of Elias Howe's 1845 machine using a curved eye-pointed needle.

257. Point de Gaze lace is used in this late nineteenth century Austrian Imperial bridal veil made for the Belgian royal family and used later by Austrian royalty. The mid-nineteenth century lace collar (below) is of needlepoint and bobbin lace.

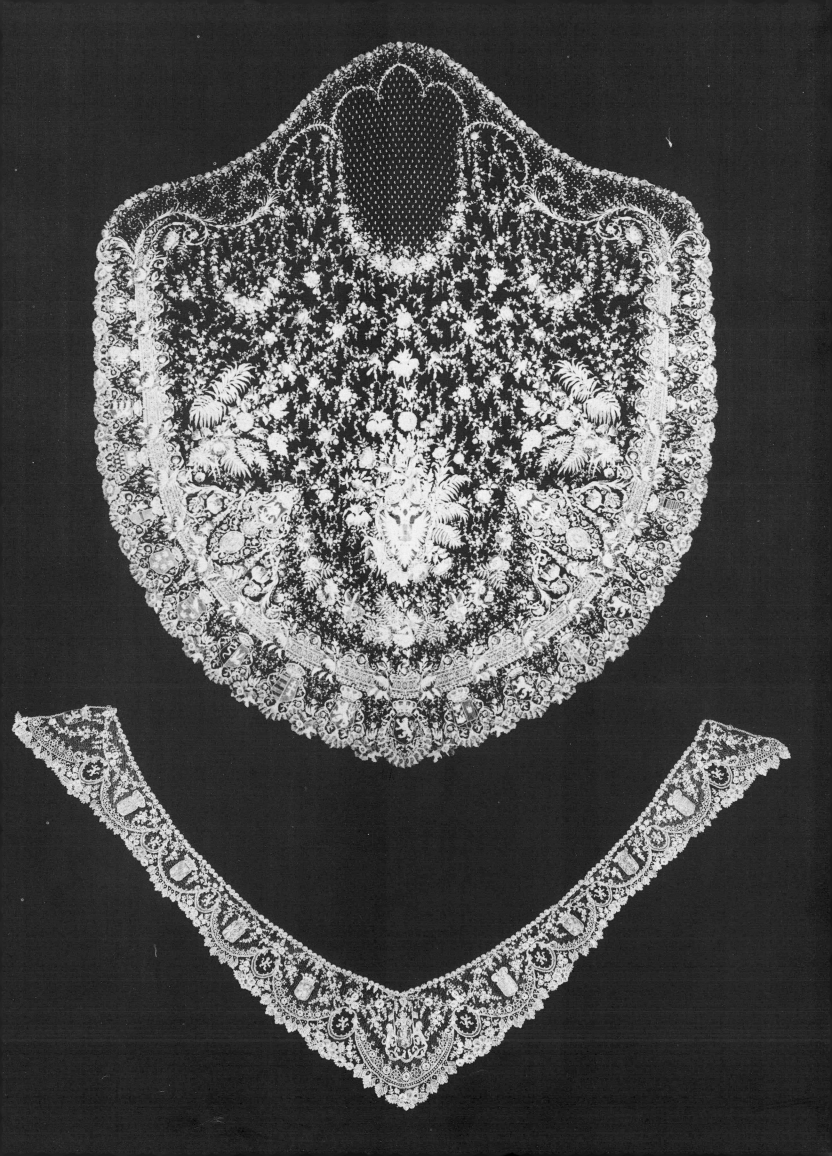

MEDICINE

259

A LARGE COLLECTION of *materia medica* came to the Smithsonian Institution from the Centennial Exhibition in Philadelphia. By 1886 the Materia Medica was listed as a division of the Department of Anthropology. By 1911 the collection had grown to include material from many branches of the medical profession.

258. The Old World apothecary shop dating in part back to the sixteenth century contains jars of drugs, books of *materia medica*, instruments, and utensils for concocting medicines, as was typical of the times. On the wall are stuffed turtles and an alligator.

259. Wintergreen is the distilled oil of a plant of eastern North America.

260. Xanthorylum, or prickly ash bark, was a favorite household remedy of toothache, rheumatism, and colic.

261. Frankincense, the gum resin of a tree found in southern Arabia and Somalia, is mentioned in an Egyptian papyrus thirty-six centuries old.

262. Copper luster or "golden" pottery is the best known pottery from Valencia, Spain, during the period of Moorish ascendancy. On the left is a Valencian lusterware albarello from around A.D. 420 to A.D. 450. The Valencia albarello on the right is sixteenth century.

263. Art and the history of drugs are combined in the Smithsonian's collection of drug jars through the ages. On the left is an ancient Egyptian alabaster Khol pot of the 18th Dynasty. In the center is a Greek lekythos of around 500 B.C. The Greco-Roman ewer of around 300 B.C. held drugs.

264. The eighteenth century Dutch delft bottle is labeled "Water of Hyssop."

262

263

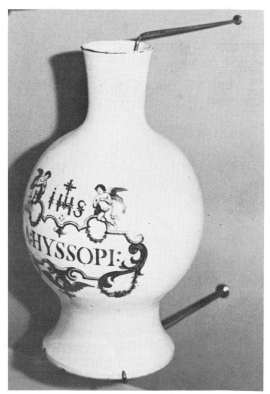

264

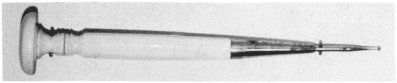

265

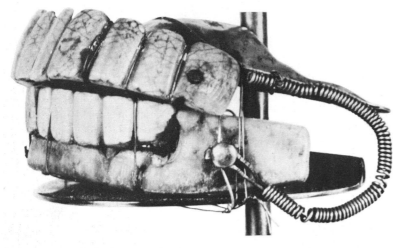

266

267

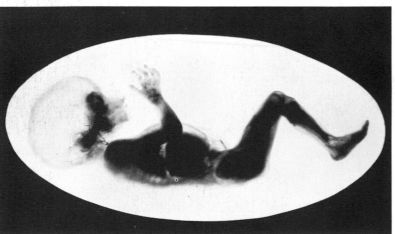

265. Shown is a nineteenth century revolving-socket hand drill.

266. Almost all fields of endeavor have felt the impact of Yankee ingenuity, and the primitive dental techniques of the eighteenth century presented a special challenge to the American inventive spirit. Many improvements have been developed since George Washington wore these false teeth.

267. Bleeding was considered a good spring tonic in the eighteenth and nineteenth centuries. This German barber's bleeding set includes cupping apparatus, instruments for pulling teeth, and a pack of cards to keep the patient amused.

268. Lighted from below, the body structure of this seven-month embryo is clearly visible.

269. Charles E. Lindbergh, famous for his 1927 nonstop flight to Paris, and Nobel prize winner Alexis Carrel, invented this Lindbergh-Carrel pump in 1935. It was used to keep alive organs removed from living bodies. The whole living organism is placed in the slanted glass tube. Pulsating gas pressure drives nutrient fluid from the lowest chamber to the organ. The pump protects the organ from bacterial infection and can keep it alive indefinitely.

270. Penicillin samples such as these were used in the first human tests at Oxford.

271. The internal workings of the human body are clearly illustrated as the vital organs light up in this transparent woman.

272. Blood pressure was first measured in 1733 when a tube was inserted directly into an animal's bloodstream. Poiseville of France first used a mercury manometer to measure blood pressure, thus leading to a series of advances that resulted in the instruments used today.

The plethysmograph is based on an apparatus described by Marey in 1876. The forearm was placed in the glass cylinder which was filled with water under pressure.

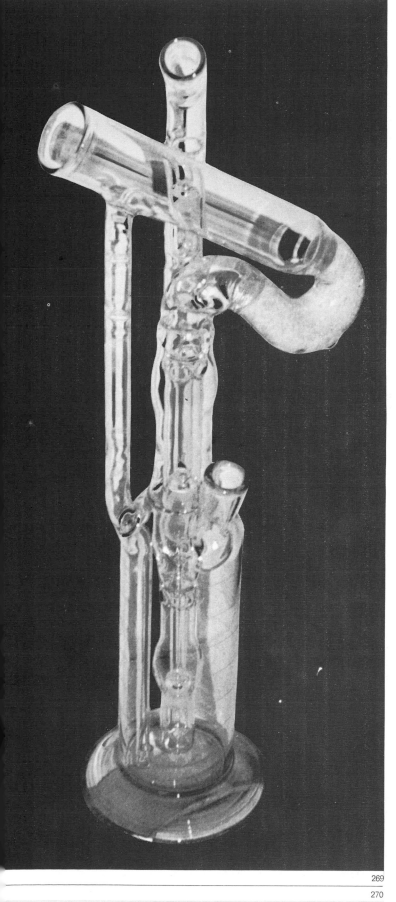

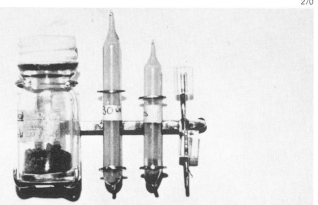

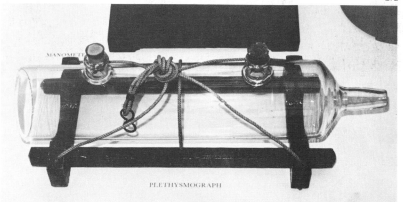

NATIONAL ZOOLOGICAL PARK

273

273. The beautiful white tiger, Mohini Rewa, Enchantress of Rewa, is not an albino but the result of a natural mutation. She was born in the province of Rewa in India, the only place where white tigers are found.

WITH THE SENSELESS slaughter in the West of great numbers of buffalo, this important North American mammal was rapidly facing extinction. Dr. Samuel Pierpont Langley, third secretary of the Institution, and other naturalists and conservationists, realized that something had to be done or the mounted specimens in Natural History exhibitions would be all that soon would remain of this symbol of the American West. Thus a small group of living animals, including buffalo and deer, were gathered together at the National Museum. The first part of this collection was received from the West in 1887 and was housed in a low building on the south side of the Smithsonian building.

Dr. Langley was influential in persuading Congress to establish the National Zoological Park in 1889. The next year it was placed under the direction of the Smithsonian.

In 1891 the animals were transferred from their cages on the Mall to a wooded area in what is now Rock Creek Park.

Many of the zoo's animals, which now number 2,800, were gifts to Presidents of the United States from foreign rulers and diplomats, a custom started by President Theodore Roosevelt, who turned over to the zoo the two baboons, a lion, and an ostrich that had been given to him by the Emperor of Ethiopia.

274

ASTROPHYSICAL OBSERVATORY

I
N THE EIGHTEEN YEARS that Samuel Pierpont Langley was secretary of the Smithsonian, the Institution began to look in many new directions. His interest in preserving those North American mammals that were fast disappearing resulted in the establishing of the zoo and his interest in astronomy resulted in the Astrophysical Observatory, established in 1890 and now playing an increasingly critical role in the study of space.

Langley said that the purpose of the Observatory was to find out how the sun "affects the earth and the wants of man on it; how the heat is distributed, and how it, in fact, affects not only the seasons and the farmer's crops, but the whole system of living things on the earth." One of the Observatory's first projects used the *bolometer,* a very sensitive thermometer which records extremely small changes in temperature and can measure radiant energy. The bolometer, which had been invented by Langley, led to many important discoveries pertaining to solar radiation.

The Observatory was first housed in a wooden structure south of the Smithsonian building. It received financial support from Alexander Graham Bell, inventor of the telephone, among others.

274. Dr. Langley with his telescope.

275

LANGLEY WAS ALSO interested in the fine arts. Until his time art had been more of a sideline with the Institution. After the great fire of 1865, which had destroyed so many of Smithson's papers and a large percentage of the art treasures collected over the years, all paintings, prints, and other objects in the field of the fine arts were housed in the Corcoran Gallery of Art in Washington or in the Library of Congress. When a great many works of art came to the Institution from the Philadelphia Centennial, interest in the arts was revived, and in 1896 the Smithsonian recalled its art treasures from the Corcoran Gallery and the Library of Congress. A large room in the east wing of the Smithsonian Institution building was made into an art gallery.

In 1904, when the Institution's art collections were established as the National Gallery of Art, the collection of Harriet Lane Johnson, who had served as First Lady for her uncle, James Buchanan, came to the Smithsonian. Many other patrons added their collections to the National Gallery, with Andrew W. Mellon giving to the nation in 1937 his tremendous art collection and a multi-million dollar building to house it. The Widener, Kress, and Dale collections later enriched it. The new museum building was given the name *National Gallery of Art,* with the other collections being known as the *National Collection of Fine Arts.*

The handsome building recently vacated when the Patent Office moved to larger quarters will be the fitting home of the National Collection of Fine Arts and the newly established National Portrait Gallery.

Langley also accepted Charles L. Freer's offer of his tremendous and important collection of American and Oriental art, although the formal transfer of the Freer collection did not take place until after his death.

276

275. *Moonlight,* by Albert Pinkham Ryder, 1847-1917.
276. *Portrait of B. Wertheimer,* by John Singer Sargent, 1856–1925.

FREER GALLERY OF ART

THE FOURTH GREAT museum building of the Smithsonian group was the gift of one man to the American people. Charles L. Freer, having made his fortune in railroads, retired at the age of forty-four to devote his time to his art collections.

Much of the Oriental sculpture, painting, porcelains and bronzes Freer collected during his travels to study the art of the Far East.

The Freer Gallery, built according to his wishes, opened to the public in 1923. In it, along with his extensive Oriental collections, are works by many of the great American painters, particularly those of Freer's personal friend, James McNeill Whistler.

Under the terms set down by Freer, the gallery can accept no gifts or loans. Purchases can be art from the Near or Far East only.

277

277. The Buddha Shakyamuni, in the style of the Six Dynasties, probably carved in the Chin Dynasty, A.D. 1115-1235.

278. Bronze figure of acrobat and bear, Chinese late Chou Dynasty, sixth to fifth centuries B.C. The figure is about six inches high.

279. Bronze ceremonial vessel, type *huo*, Chinese early Chou Dynasty, twelfth or eleventh century B.C.

280. Bronze ceremonial vessel of the type *li-ting*, Chinese Shang Dynasty, thirteenth and twelfth centuries B.C.

281. Bronze quadruped, Chinese late Chou Dynasty, sixth to fourth centuries B.C.

278

279

280

281

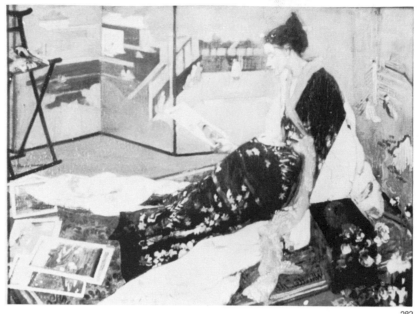

282

282. *Caprice in Purple and Gold, No. 2, The Golden Screen,*
American, by James McNeill Whistler, 1834–1903.

283. *Sailor and His Sweetheart,*
American, by Gari Melchers, 1860–1932.

283

NATURAL HISTORY MUSEUM

284. The Natural History Museum.

ALTHOUGH LANGLEY had been secretary at the time of the ground breaking ceremonies for the third great building of the Smithsonian group, Charles Doolittle Walcott had become the fourth secretary by the time the cornerstone was laid. Known at the time as the United States National Museum, it is now the Natural History Museum (284). Portions of the building were opened to the public in 1910, the building being completed a year later. Its octagonal rotunda is eighty feet in diameter and 124½ feet in height. The four acres of floor space provided room for both exhibitions and study collections. But as the National Museum expanded its collections, crowded conditions resulted.

With new wings added in the 1960's and the removal to the Museum of History and Technology of the cultural history items long housed side by side with the natural history collections, the building once again is dedicated to the exhibiting and study of the natural sciences.

285

LATIN AMERICAN ARCHAEOLOGY

SYMBOLIZED BY THE huge calendar stone representing the Aztec conception of the universe, the ancient civilizations of Latin America flourished and died during the medieval centuries of Europe. From Peru, where the Incas established one of the world's greatest cultures, northward to the Valley of Mexico, which was ruled by the Aztecs at the time of the Spanish conquest, the earth is rich with the archaeological remains of artistic and practical peoples.

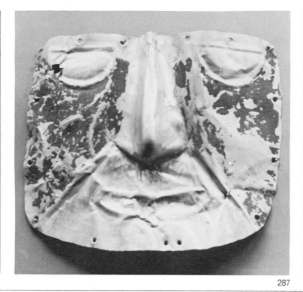

286

287

288

290

289

285. Shown here is a full-size reproduction of a twelve-foot diameter Aztec calendar stone dating from A.D. 1479.

286, 287, 288. Precious metals were worked with great skill by the Andean craftsmen who made the cast spoon, the Chimu mummy mask of hammered gold, and the Inca cast-silver llamas.

289. This stone ceremonial seat from Manabi, Ecuador, is probably pre-Inca, dating before A.D. 1300.

290. This unique straw figure found in a grave of about A.D. 1100 is wearing its original costume, typical of prehistoric men of Peru.

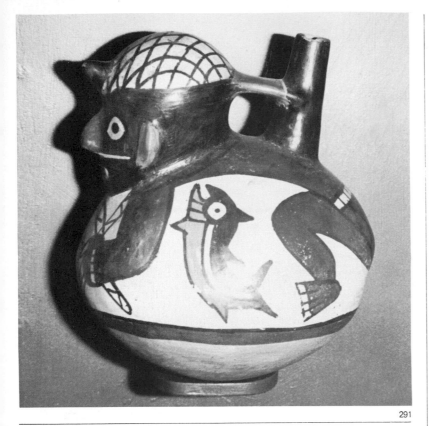

291

294

292

293

295

296

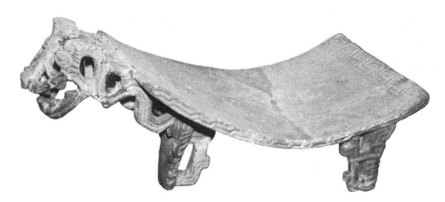

298

297

291, 292, 293, 294. The art of pottery-making was highly developed in ancient Peru as shown by the unique Nasca vessel with handle, the grinning face of the Tiahuanaco vase, the elaborately painted Mochica vessels, and the unusual Inca bird plate.

295. Jadeite from which this amulet was carved was acquired by trade with the Indians to the north and apparently was treasured more highly than gold.

296. The Marajoara people established a settlement on an island at the mouth of the Amazon River but declined and disappeared before A.D. 1500. They put the bones of their deceased in jars like this one and buried them in cemetery mounds.

297. A Quimbaya seated figure from Colombia.

298. Typical of the basic culture of Central America is this stone ceremonial stool.

299. The first permanent European settlement in the New World was established among the Arawak Indians of the Antilles, who made this stone ceremonial ax.

300. Metals were hollow-cast by the cire perdue (lost wax) process, often used in casting zoomorphic amulets.

301. The Coclé culture of Panama used natural forms such as the animal shape of this vessel.

302. The Olmec people of southeastern Mexico sculptured monolithic stone heads of tremendous size and weight. This small stone human statue resembles in style of carving these huge heads. A ten foot high reproduction of the head found at La Venta, Mexico, is on display in the hall.

303. The bowl decoration is an example of the Coclé culture of Panama.

304. Greatly influenced by the Olmecs was the great Mayan civilization. Art, architecture, and painting reached a high point of refinement before this culture declined. The Mayans were skilled potters as is shown by this sculptured bowl.

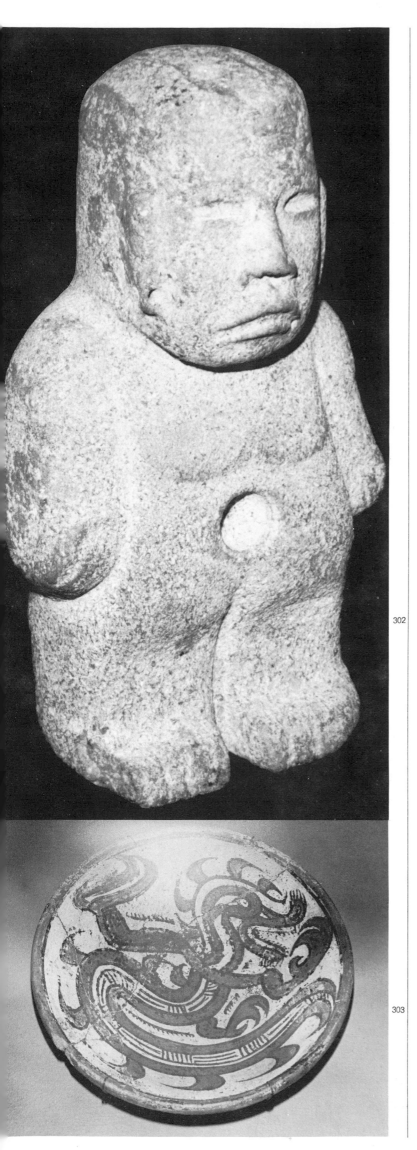

302

304

303

305

306

307

310

308

309

305, 306. Bordering the Pacific Ocean between A.D. 700 and 1200 were the Tarascan people, who gave many of their sculptures human characteristics.

307. The symbolically carved lava box held the hearts of human sacrificial victims.

308. Xochipilli, "the Flower Prince," was the god of pleasure, feasting, and frivolity.

309. Typical of Aztec ceramic art is this rattle.

310. Shown is the sacred seat of Tezcatlipoca, "smoking mirror," the chief god of the Aztecs.

311. Olmec influences are evident in the sculpture of the Zapotecs of southwestern Mexico shown on the opposite page.

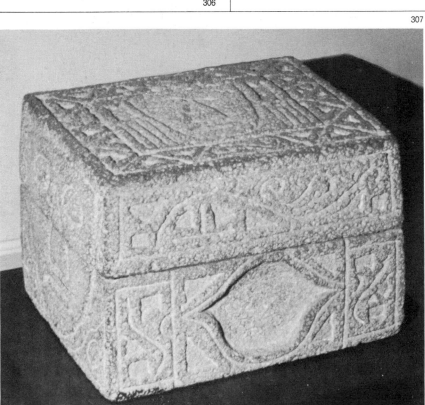

311

312

3

3

312. The "feathered serpent," god of learning
and the priesthood, was called Quetzalcoatl.

313. This Aztec carving of a seated monkey
is of mythological and ceremonial significance.

314, 315. Figurines of the Archaic or pre-classical period,
1200 B.C. to A.D. 300, were handmade. The first appearance
of mold-made figurines was in the Teotihuacan period,
A.D. 300 to 900.

316. Figurines, while not common, were mold-made during
the Toltec period, A.D. 900 to 1200.

317. Elaborate mold-made figurines characterize the Aztec
period, A.D. 1200 to 1521, the year of the Spanish conquest.

318. This head is typical of Aztec ceramic art.

319. The art of sculpture in stone reached a high point
of refinement during the Aztec period. The grasshopper
is of mythological and ceremonial significance.

314

315

316

318

319

LIFE BEGAN IN THE SEA. All living creatures were bound to a watery existence until the first amphibian crawled upon the land. The ocean depths comprise a world to themselves inhabited by animals of every kind from soft fragile jellyfish to monstrous whales. The study of the millions of species of marine plant and animal life is a never-ending process in which the rewards may be the discovery of a new food supply or evidence of an unknown prehistoric creature.

Towering over the Hall of Life in the Sea is the ninety-foot blue whale, shown as it is sounding, or diving. The sleek streamlined appearance, so different from the bloated bodies of most whales on display, is due to the animal's being shown as it would have looked under water and subjected to its pressure.

320

321

LIFE IN THE SEA

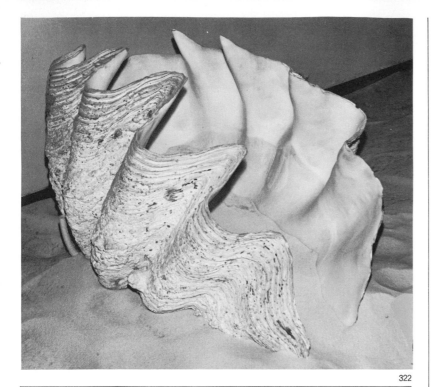

322

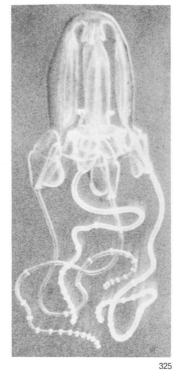

325

323

324

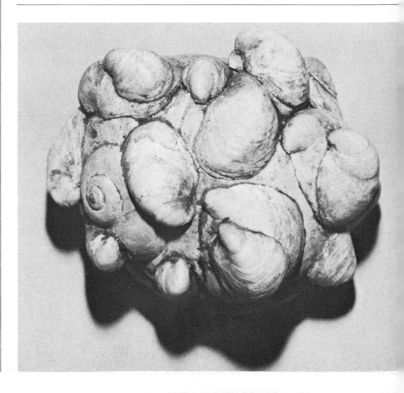

322. The giant clam closes its huge shell slowly and is not a dangerous hazard to swimmers.

323. Reef, or "lettuce leaf," coral found at Palau, Caroline Islands, in the Pacific Ocean.

324. Mollusks are the shell-producing creatures of the seas. The scorpion shell is found in the Indian and Pacific Oceans.

325. Over 90 percent of marine life is made up of invertebrates, creatures without a backbone. Because some of these animals are so small and are made up of soft gelatinous tissues, like the cubomedusan jellyfish of tropical Pacific waters, the organisms cannot be put on display except in model form and enlarged many times.

326. The paper nautilus, another example of the mollusk, is found in warm seas all over the world.

327. Another example of the mollusk is the *Crepidula fornicata*, which lives along the Atlantic coast from Nova Scotia to Texas.

328. Another example of reef, or "lettuce leaf" coral, *Pectinia alcicornis*, also from the Caroline Islands.

328

GOOSEFISH
Lophius americanus

OSTEOLOGY

COMPARATIVE ANATOMY is the science which compares different classes of fishes and quadrupeds with one another. Much of mankind's knowledge of medicine, biology, heredity, and genetics is based on observations made from such comparisons.

Although the science of osteology, the comparison of bones and complete skeletons, is not new, the display of such skeletons compared with one another is new. The bones are attached so that the skeletons in the exhibit appear in the same relation to one another that they had when the animal was alive.

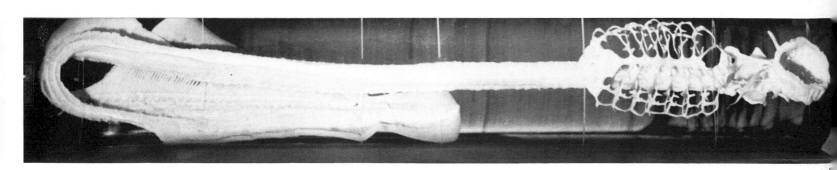

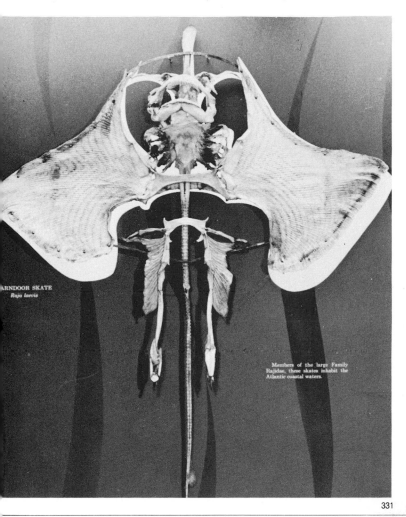

BARNDOOR SKATE
Raja laevis

Members of the large Family
Rajidae, these skates inhabit the
Atlantic coastal waters.

329. The skeleton of the goosefish reflects the ferocious
appearance of the fish itself. One of the anglerfishes,
the goosefish has a fin spine, called the illicium, on top
of the head (circled on the drawing), which serves
as a fishing pole with a bait and is used to attract
the smaller fishes which are its food.

330. The sea lamprey goes upstream to spawn. The open,
disk-shaped mouth has numerous horny teeth for rasping flesh.

331. Inhabiting the Atlantic coastal waters is the barndoor
skate. The enlarged pectoral fins are attached to the head
and are supported by radial cartilages. Some rays swim
forward by front-to-rear undulating movements of the fins.

332. Flatfishes are found along the shores and continental
slopes of all seas north of the Antarctic Circle. A few can
be found in fresh water. These bottom-dwellers are unique
among fishes because both their eyes are on the same
side of the head. They swim with their eyeless, colorless
side down. On the left is the right-eyed flounder, sometimes
incorrectly called the sole, another of the flatfish.

333. Spending most of their time swimming on or under
water or flying over it are the four groups of aquatic birds.
At the top is the grebe, beneath it the loon, and on the right
the aquatic penguin and the smaller shearwater. The loon
is a foot-propelled swimmer with webbed toes.

331

RIGHT-EYED FLOUNDER
(Family Pleuronectidae)

The right-eyed flounders, which nor-
mally have their eyes on the right side,
are described as dextral. Sometimes
these fishes are incorrectly called soles,
but soles (Family Soleidae) are another
of flatfishes with eyes either on
left side and scales on the

332

333

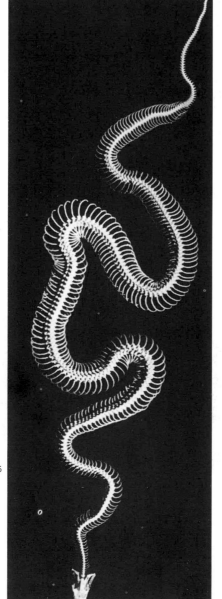

335

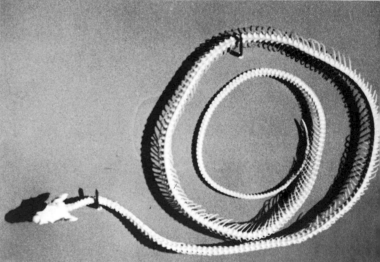

334, 335, 336. Three families of snakes include most of those that are poisonous. Russell's viper, of Asia (top), is of the Viperidae family. The boa constrictor (left) is of the snake family Boidae, which is known for large size and the traces of hind limbs that have not completely disappeared. The slug-eating snake lives in tropical America.

337. The Egyptian cobra of Africa is of the Elapidae family. The third poisonous family is the Hydrophidae.

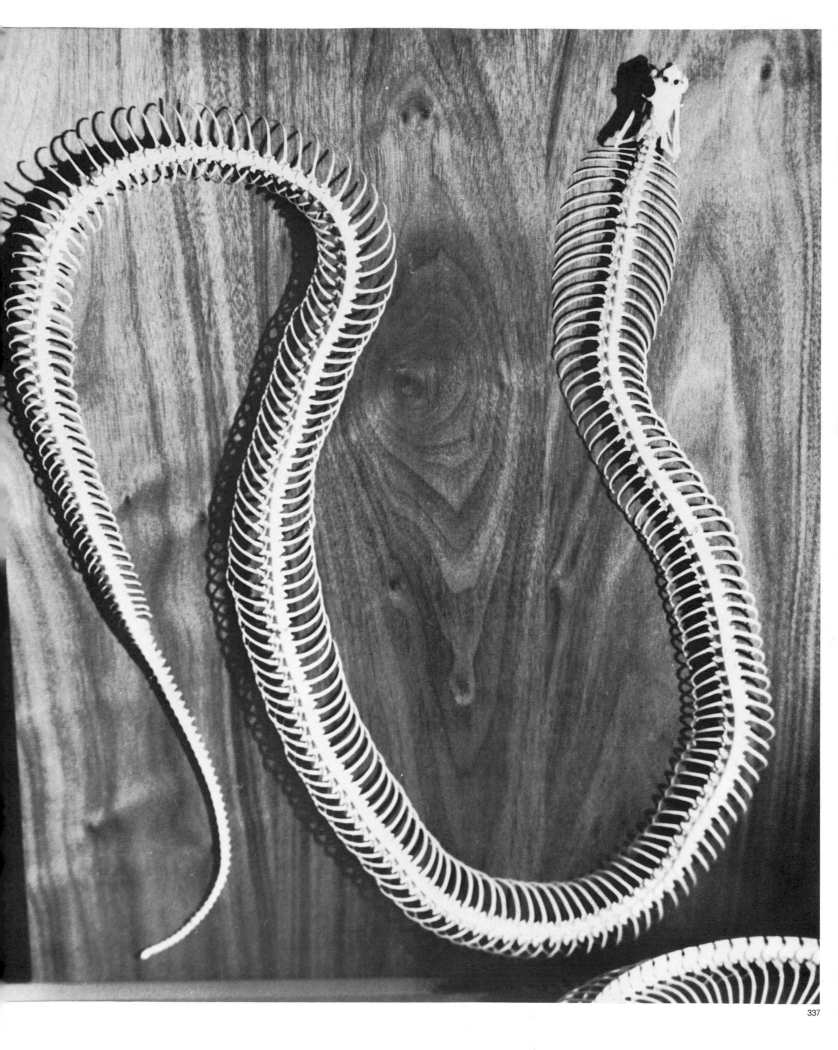

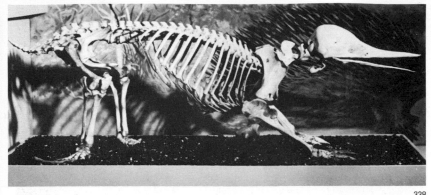

338

339

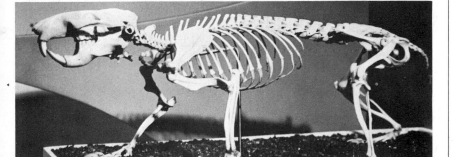

340

341

342

338. The echidna has massive limbs and claws for digging in hard ground. It is an anteater with a long toothless skull.

339. The platypus has a flat body modified for aquatic life. Its feet are webbed and its bill is used to grub for worms in freshwater ponds.

340. The insectivores are primitive mammals that may represent the ancestors of the more advanced bats, carnivores, and primates. The present-day insectivores are all small like the mole, found in the United States.

341. Close to the insectivores is the tree shrew, a small squirrel-like animal of Malay that is active only in the daylight.

342. The mountain beaver is the most primitive living rodent.

343. The Samoan fruit bat is also known as a flying fox because of its foxlike head. It feeds only on fruit.

344. The three-toed sloth is of the edentates order.

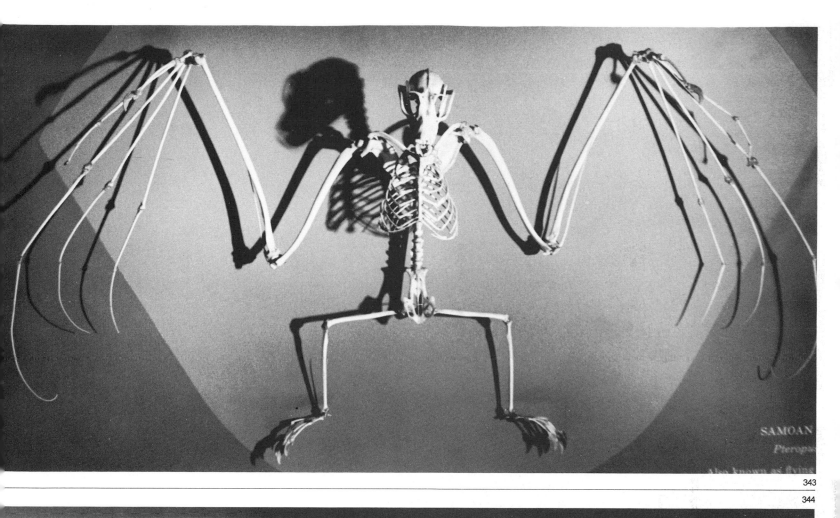

SAMOAN
Pteropus
also known as flying

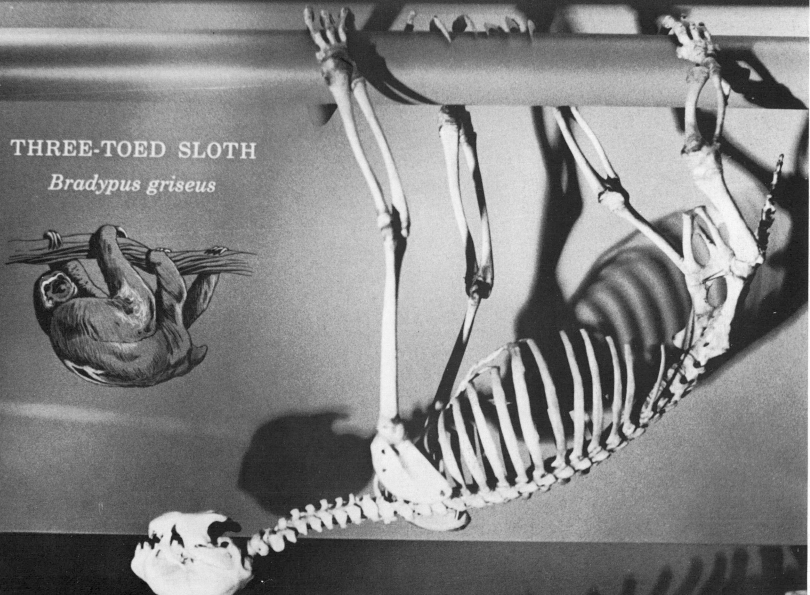

THREE-TOED SLOTH
Bradypus griseus

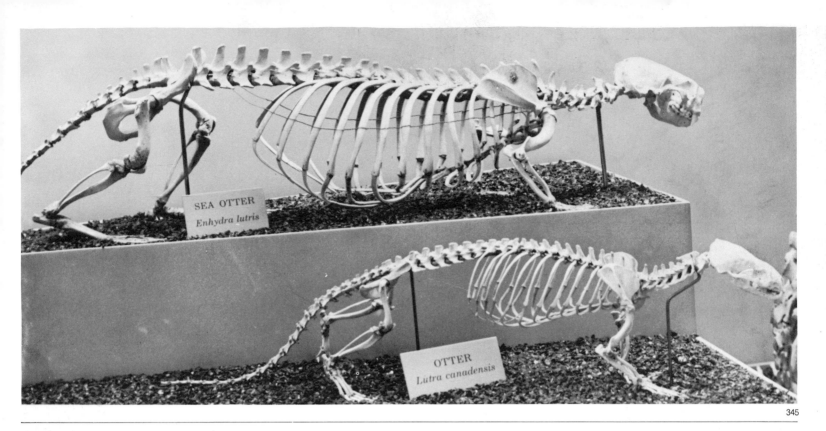

SEA OTTER
Enhydra lutris

OTTER
Lutra canadensis

345

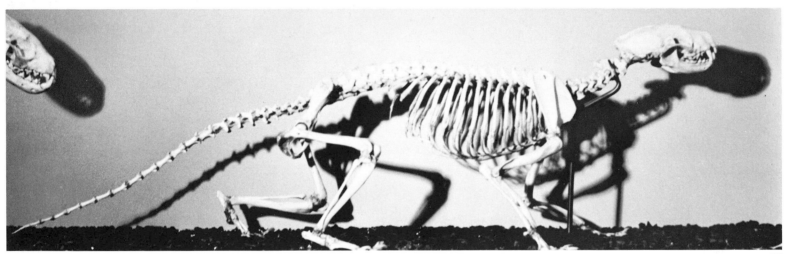

346

347

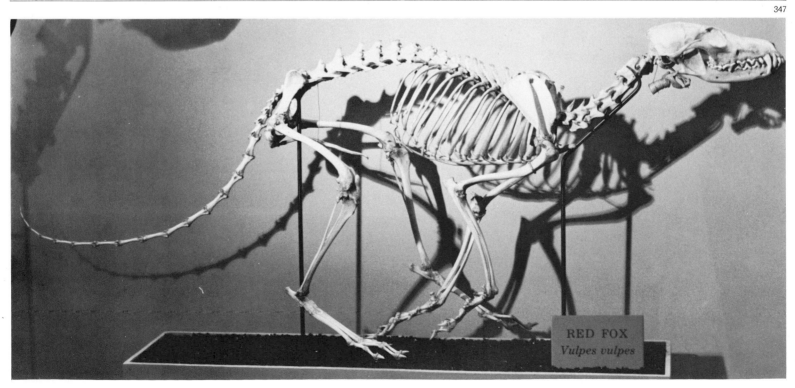

RED FOX
Vulpes vulpes

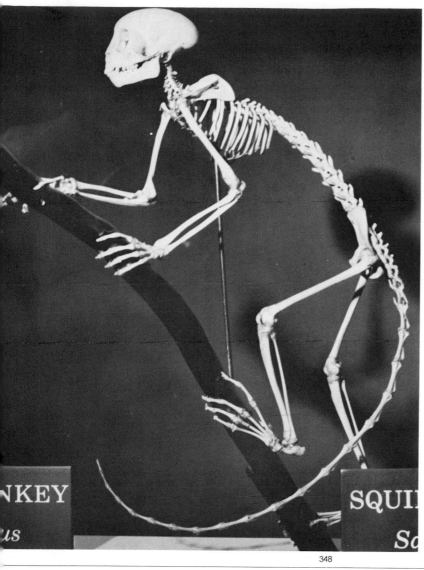

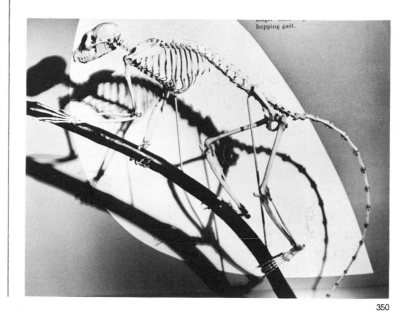

345. The otter (opposite page, top) is representative of the carnivores. The aquatic otter, such as the sea otter above, is a distinct subgroup from which the true seal may have developed.

346. Although the striped skunk (opposite page, center) is mild mannered, other members of the weasel family are the most ferocious of mammals, killing animals much larger than themselves.

347. The red fox (opposite page, below) and the familiar dog are canidae, of the carnivores order.

348. The majority of living primates are of three families commonly called monkeys. The squirrel monkey is shown.

349. The comparison of the homo sapiens on the left and the gorilla is made by the living homo sapiens standing in front of the exhibit.

350. The lemur, found only on the island of Madagascar, is the modern survivor of the primitive primates. It runs on tree branches and the ground on all four feet.

351

AFRICA

PRIMITIVE MAN probably had his beginnings on the African continent as far back as two million years ago. If so, the cultures of that dark land have a longer history than anywhere else in the world. Considering the time span covered, western nations have known and still know very little about the people of Africa other than the northern part which is adjacent to the sea and has always been a part of the Mediterranean civilization. Only recently have anthropologists and other scientists turned to the study of what is known as Negro Africa.

Negro Africa can be divided culturally into four broad regions: East, Central, West, and South, each section having spawned societies that only now are coming into their own and taking their places with the nations of the world. Now more than ever, the people of Europe and the Americas need to know and understand the background and cultures of these peoples who will play an increasingly important role in world affairs.

352

351. Men of Ibibio wore this type of mask to impersonate ancestors assigned to ghosthood.

352. A good luck fetish or portrait figure such as this Ivory Coast figurine was a reminder of a good friend. Individuals were distinguished by facial features and by scarification patterns.

353   354

353. Excellent workmanship and design are incorporated in this Kuba dance knife.

354. North Africa is the heart of the Moslem world. For centuries the curved double-edged jambiya (Arab knife) has been considered an excellent fighting weapon and is still in use. The one shown (above, right) is from Morocco.

355. Mangbetu chiefs used this copper knife as a scepter, as shown in the drawing of the Mangbetu chief of 1870.

356. The sheath of this East African sword is inlaid with ivory.

357. Symbol of judicial power was this Bangi chief's ax.

358. Iron objects, such as this throwing knife from the Congo, are some of the many types of money used in West Africa.

KING OF THE MANGBETU

(About 1870)

355

356

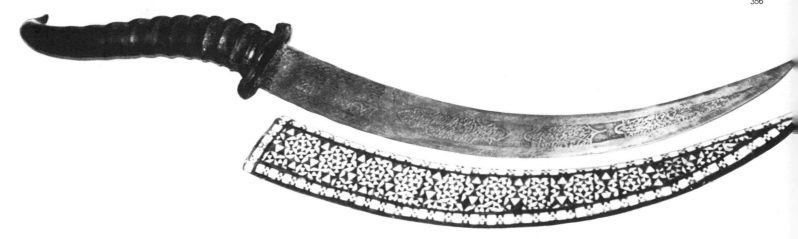

357

358

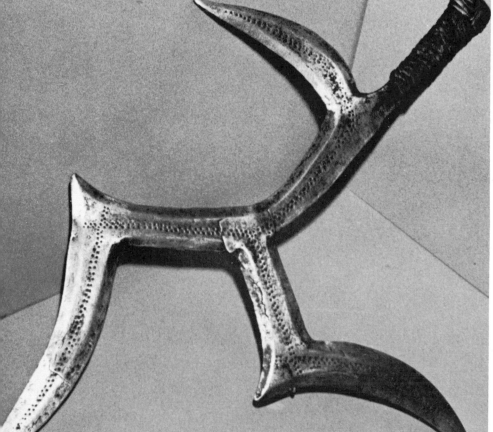

359

360

359. West African brasswork is some of the finest known. The brasswork of the Benin is divided into three periods. The original of this early period head of the Queen Mother, cast in the fifteenth century, is in the British Museum.

360. This original casting of a memorial head is from the Benin middle period.

361. "The Destroyers" is a powerful secret society of Ibibio. This spirit figure represents the son of the mythical founder of the society.

362. Used as entertainment at funerals, this dance mask is from Gola.

361

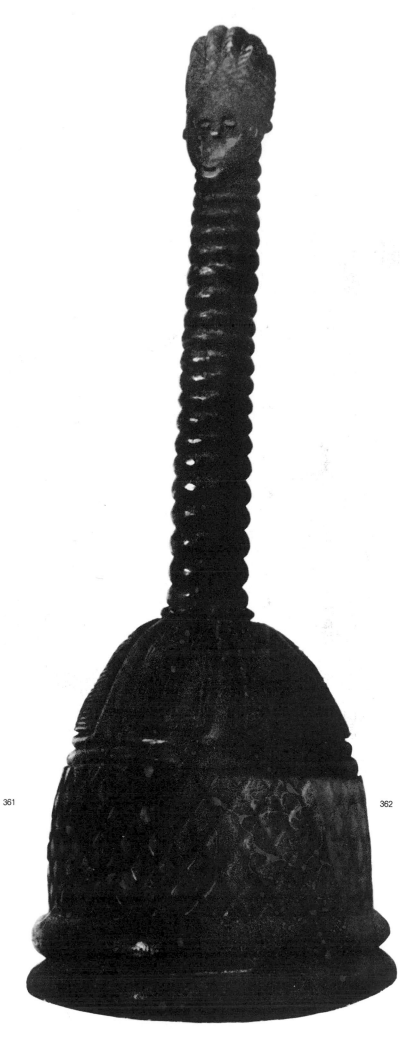

362

AIR AND SPACE

363

363. The new Smithsonian Air and Space Museum will be 97 feet high and 734 feet long and will display many complete aircraft.

364. Shown is a scale model of the proposed National Air Museum.

O RIGINALLY BUILT in 1917 as a testing laboratory for Liberty aircraft engines, the building that is the present Air and Space Museum was acquired by the Smithsonian in 1919 and opened to the public in 1920. In the restricted space available is a comprehensive history of flight from the theories of Da Vinci to the space capsules. Besides models of many kinds of aircraft of many countries, there are examples of smaller equipment associated with historic flights of the past, and four of the historic aircraft themselves.

Soon to be constructed on the Mall is the Smithsonian's new Air and Space Museum building. By an ingenious combination of exhibit levels suspended between great columns and the use of large areas of glass, the architect, Gyo Obata, will provide a building with a flexibility which will permit the display of objects ranging from subminiaturized instruments up to very large complete aircraft, space vehicles, and rocket boosters.

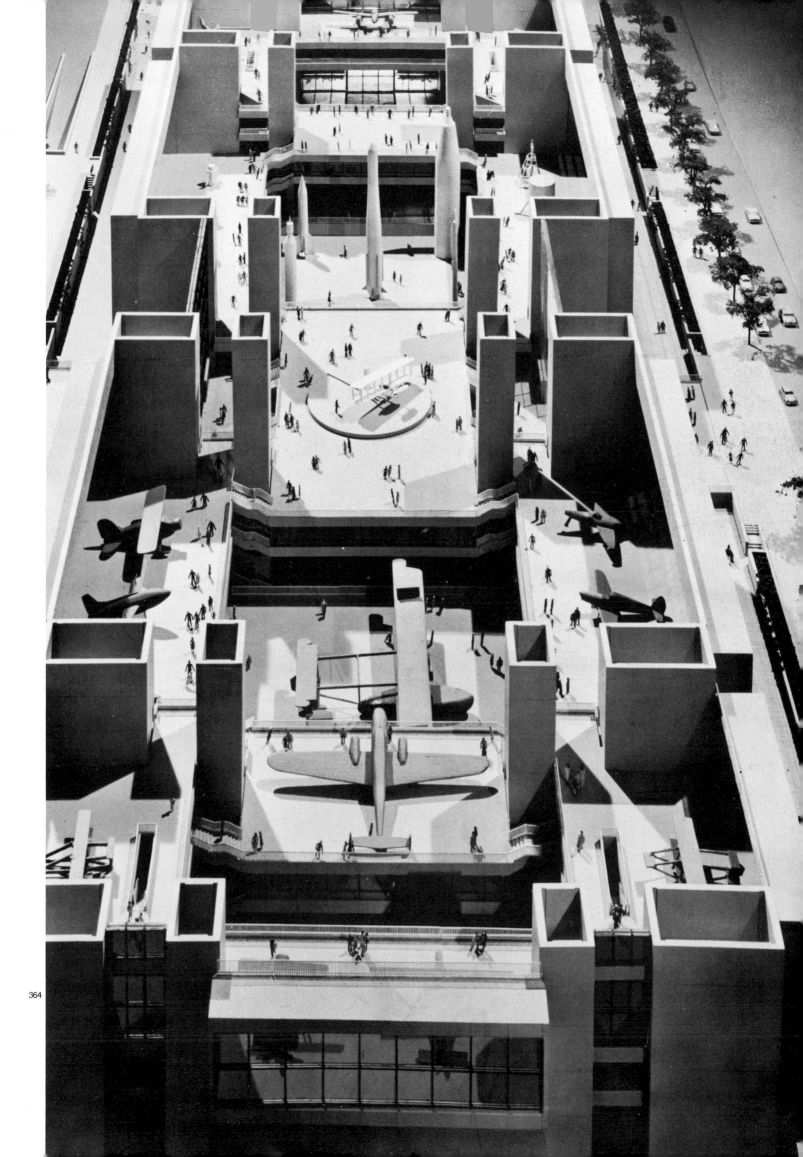

365

366

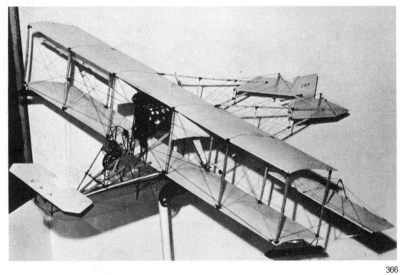

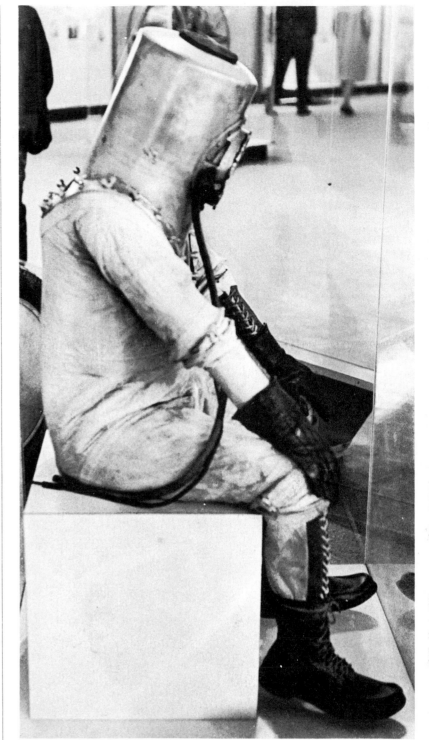

369

365. Anchored to what might be considered the first aircraft carrier, the flat-topped *George Washington Parke Custis*, is the observation balloon used to observe the Confederate blockade at Budds Ferry, November, 1861. Shown is a contemporary watercolor.

366. In 1911 the U.S. Navy acquired its first aircraft, shown by this model. Built by Glenn H. Curtiss, it carried two people.

367. The most famous airplane in the collection is the "Spirit of St. Louis" which carried Charles A. Lindbergh nonstop from New York to Paris in 1927. The plane was flown to the Smithsonian by Lindbergh himself and put on display in 1928. Years later Charles Lindbergh visited the Smithsonian and climbed back into the cockpit of the plane in order to refresh his memory for the book he was writing about his nonstop flight across the Atlantic.

368. In 1926 another first took place which was to lead to many more of historic importance. Dr. Robert Goddard successfully launched the first liquid-fueled rocket at Auburn, Massachusetts. His rocket, shown in the photograph with Goddard himself, contained the basic configuration and essential elements of modern rockets.

369. This Wright "Whirlwind" J-5 engine of 1928 was the center engine in the Fokker C-2 that completed a refueled duration flight of 150 hours, 40 minutes, and 15 seconds.

370. The first pressurized flying suit was worn in 1934 by Wiley Post during high altitude tests in the "Winnie Mae".

371. In 1955 the U.S. Army was experimenting with the Hiller Flying Platform.

370

371

372

373

372. The "Friendship 7" is the Mercury space capsule in which Colonel John H. Glenn became the first American to orbit the earth, February 20, 1962. The capsule orbited the earth three times.

373. Able, the Rhesus monkey who was launched 300 miles into space by a Jupiter rocket in May, 1959, is shown in original bio-capsule and cradle. Able died the day after her successful flight from causes having nothing to do with the flight. Baker, a squirrel monkey launched into space with Able, is alive and well and can be seen at the National Zoological Park.

374. Placed into orbit around the earth in December, 1958, the Atlas rocket-powered missile broadcast President Eisenhower's goodwill message to the world. The missile is 75 feet 10 inches in height.

152

NATIONAL GALLERY OF ART

CONSIDERED BY many people to be the most beautiful building in Washington, the pale pink marble museum that is probably the largest all marble structure in the world houses one of the world's finest art collections.

Charles G. Abbott was the secretary of the Smithsonian Institution when in 1936 Andrew Mellon gave to the American people his fifty million dollar art collection and a ten million dollar museum building. The Gallery was not finished when Samuel Kress donated his magnificent Italian collection. Since the museum opened in 1941, other famous collectors have increased the breadth and scope of its contents.

375. *The Adoration of the Magi*
Botticelli
Andrew Mellon Collection

376. *Portrait of a Lady with an Ostrich-Feather Fan*
Rembrandt
Widener Collection

377. *Laocoön*
El Greco
Samuel H. Kress Collection

376

377

378. *Mrs. Richard Yates*
Gilbert Stuart
Andrew Mellon Collection

379. *Mortlake Terrace*
Joseph Mallord William Turner
Andrew Mellon Collection

380. *Campo San Zanipolo*
Francesco Guardi
Samuel H. Kress Collection

378

379

381

382

383

381. *The Lovers*
Pablo Picasso
Chester Dale Collection

382. *New England Village*
Artist Unknown
Gift of Edgar William and Bernice Chrysler Garbisch

383. *Agostina*
Jean-Baptiste-Camille Corot
Chester Dale Collection

SMITHSONIAN TROPICAL RESEARCH INSTITUTE

AFTER A PERIOD of quiescence necessitated by the depression years and the concentration of its efforts on the war program during World War II, the Smithsonian Institution once again returned to its educational and scientific pursuits under the direction of its sixth secretary, Alexander Wetmore, the second ornithologist of renown to assume that position.

Although its interests have always been world wide, the physical boundaries of the Institution centered in the District of Columbia, with only the Astrophysical Observatory in Cambridge, Massachusetts, out of that area. In 1946, the institution, under Dr. Wetmore, expanded to include the Canal Zone Biological Area on Barro Colorado Island in the Panama Canal Zone. This tropical plant and wildlife sanctuary, six miles square in Gatun Lake, is for the use of Smithsonian scientists and is visited by authorities in the field of natural sciences from all over the world. It is the only tropical scientific research station of its kind in the Western Hemisphere. It was renamed the Smithsonian Tropical Research Institute in 1966.

The second great event that occurred under Dr. Wetmore's secretaryship was the centennial celebration in August, 1946, of the founding of the Institution. A commemorative three-cent postage stamp was issued showing the first Smithsonian building.

MUSEUM OF HISTORY AND TECHNOLOGY

384

384. The Museum of History and Technology of the Smithsonian Institution.

385. Dominating the main lobby of the Museum of History and Technology is the Star-Spangled Banner, the flag that flew over Fort McHenry on the 13th and the morning of the 14th of September, 1814, during the attack on Baltimore, Maryland. This is the flag that inspired Francis Scott Key to write the poem that is now the National Anthem. Originally thirty by forty-two feet in size, the lower portion was given away as souvenirs long before coming to the Smithsonian Institution.

385

386. Similar to the bombs that pierced the Star-Spangled Banner during the battle, this 13-inch bomb was fired at American troops at an earlier time by one of the ships that took part in the bombardment of Fort McHenry.

THE ARTS AND INDUSTRIES BUILDING did little to alleviate the crowded conditions that had developed within the Smithsonian Institution in its first years. The long awaited spacious quarters of the United States National Museum, now called the Museum of Natural History, also proved inadequate within a few years of its opening in 1911. In 1939, years before the one hundredth anniversary of the founding of the institution, it was obvious that a new building was needed. Under the direction of Leonard Carmichael, the seventh secretary, the fifth Smithsonian museum building became a reality.

Opened in 1964, the Museum of History and Technology made possible exhibit halls designed to incorporate the newest techniques of display. At last under one roof were the historical, cultural, and technical treasures of the United States.

With American history symbolized by the original Star-Spangled Banner, and technology by the Foucoult Pendulum, a golden ball at the end of a cord four stories long, the newest museum of the Smithsonian complex houses in its eight acres of floor space such things as the giant machines of industry and the fragile clothing of the nation's founders and leaders.

Long before the ground breaking ceremonies for the new building in 1959, Smithsonian curators and exhibit specialists were hard at work planning, constructing, and storing the new exhibits. Thousands of labels were being written and edited to identify the objects that would be put on display years later. The building was opened to the public with only about one quarter of the exhibits on view. Installation of the choicest items from the historical and technological collections goes on as more and more exhibit halls are completed.

Besides three huge floors of exhibits, the building contains curators' offices and the research collections and storage rooms. The most modern equipment protects the precious objects and provides comfort for the millions of people who yearly come to see and learn new aspects of the American heritage as illustrated by the treasures of the American nation.

387. The Foucault pendulum swings above the marble compass rose set into the lobby floor. Each morning the ball of the pendulum is started swinging in the direction of the gold pointer. During the day the rotation of the earth moves the pointer away from the swing of the pendulum. Although apparently the pendulum ball changes direction, in reality it is the floor beneath it that moves as the earth rotates. The pendulum is swung by a motor in order to exaggerate the pendulum swing and show the change of direction more clearly.

388. The great locomotive on display in the Railroad exhibit was moved into place during the early stages of the construction of the building.

389. Probably the most important example of American classical revival sculpture, this statue of George Washington was carved in 1840 by Horatio Greenough, the first important American sculptor. Based on the Greek statue of Zeus famous in antiquity and with a likeness fashioned after Houdon's bust of Washington in the Virginia State Capitol, Washington is shown as a symbol of American freedom.

390. The Presidential reception room is used on state occasions.

389

390

PHYSICAL SCIENCES

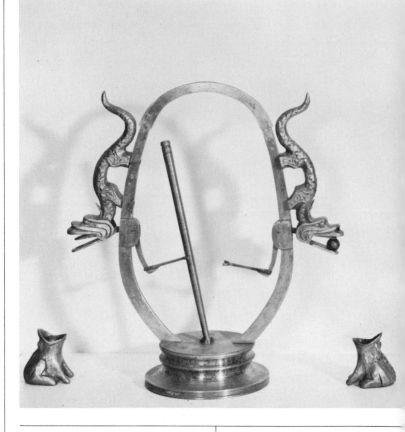

392

Technological advances have often been based on a new discovery made in one of the physical sciences. An undreamed of machine or process has, in the past, been just the practical application of an abstract theory from the realm of pure science. Exhibits and objects from this field of human knowledge are an appropriate beginning for a survey of American technology.

391. According to Chinese annals, this "seismograph" was invented in A.D. 132 by the astronomer Choko. Each dragon carries a copper ball in its mouth, delicately poised so that at the least vibration it will fall into the mouth of the toad below. When an earthquake shakes the instrument, the ball that falls indicates the direction of the earthquake.

392. This astrolabe is Italian of about 1670.

393. Also from about 1670 is this astrolabe from India.

394. In 1867 D. F. Henry invented the first water current meter to use a cup type rotator and to successfully register the rotation by electric current. This instrument won an award at the Philadelphia Centennial. Henry had used it to measure the flow of the St. Clair and Niagara Rivers.

395. Built by Jules Richard of Paris in 1890, this rain gauge registers the amount of rainfall. It was used at Mount Weather, Virginia.

396. The Wheelbarrow Odometer of 1907, an instrument for measuring distance traveled, was used in survey work in New Jersey.

396

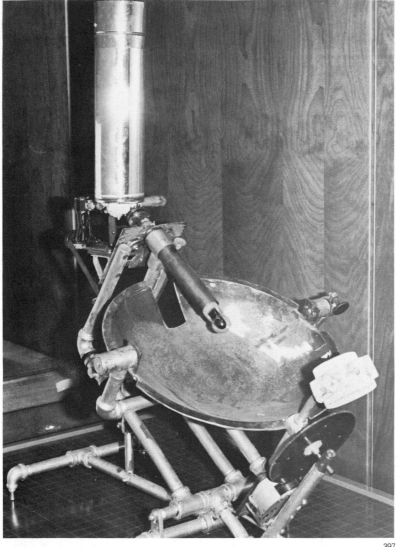

397

397. Charles G. Abbot, fifth secretary of the Smithsonian Institution, invented this solar power boiler in 1941. The machine shown is three feet high, but a larger model with a mirror ten feet in diameter would yield more than two horsepower, a fifty-foot mirror over fifty horsepower. Twenty to twenty-five percent of the energy of the solar rays intercepted by the mirror may be converted into mechanical work.

398. Prisms and reflectors of various shapes demonstrate the reflective and refractive properties of light.

399. An orrery is a machine that imitates the movement of the sun and the planets and their moons. Although the support is not the original, the orrery shown belonged to the famous English chemist, Joseph Priestley, while he lived in the United States at the end of the eighteenth century. The maker is unknown.

400. Priestley also used this globe of the world.

401. The Ramsden dividing engine of 1774 was the first of its kind. Shown is the original instrument that has been restored.

402. David Rittenhouse, a Philadelphia clockmaker, was the maker of the earliest known American-made telescopes. The first instrument of his that still exists is in the hall of the American Philosophical Society in Philadelphia, of which he was president. His 19-inch Zenith Sector is one of two in the Museum of History and Technology.

Rittenhouse made instruments principally for his own use. The telescopes owned by Washington, Jefferson, and other gentleman scholars of the day were made in Europe.

399

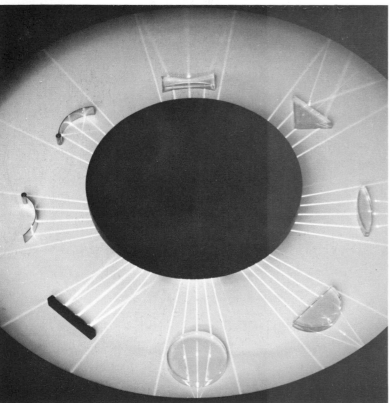

398

400

401

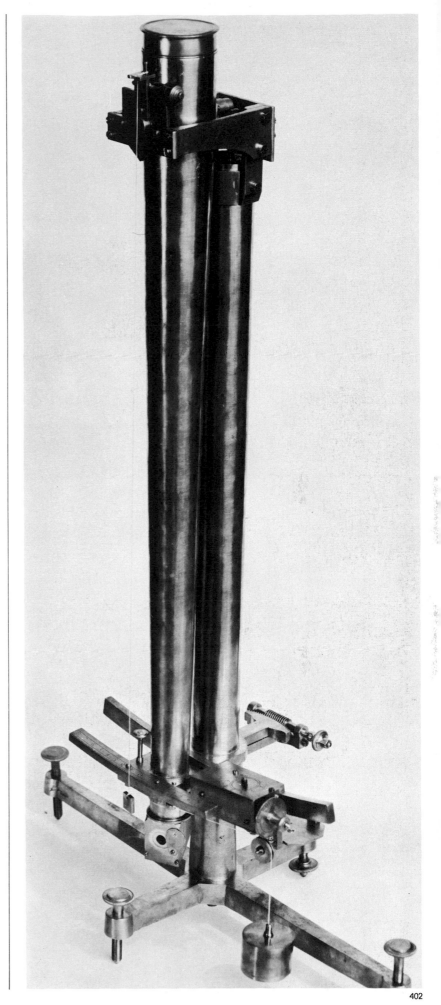

402

403. Henry Fitz was a Massachusetts instrument maker. Trained as a locksmith, he made telescopes and other instruments with components of his own design and using tools he had invented. His lenses and instruments were used by many of the leading observatories of the day. His refracting telescope is shown, lacking the stand.

404. When he died suddenly in 1863, he was planning the production of a 24-inch telescope. Soon after his death, his workshop was closed. It remained almost untouched from that date until it was transferred to the Smithsonian Institution almost a hundred years later. The contents of the shop are virtually complete with Fitz's tools, account books, and even his door key as he left them. The portrait mannikin of Henry Fitz polishes a lens in the original shop, on display in the Museum of History and Technology.

405. In 1893, at the age of seventy-three, John Peate started work on the largest telescope reflector disk in the world at the time. Shown is the 62-inch disk, which was cast to his design by the Standard Plate Glass Company in 1895. It weighs 2,500 pounds.

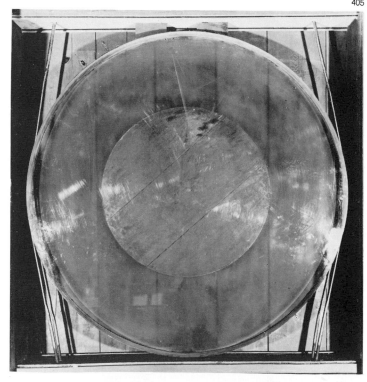

MACHINERY
AND
TOOLS

406

A HUNDRED CARLOADS of objects came to the Institution from the Philadelphia Centennial. The many industrial items gave impetus to the collection of tools and machines of all kinds. Mechanical devices from an ancient sun dial to an atomic clock tell the story of America's industrial revolution and her attainment of technical supremacy. The unique collection of patent models which was turned over to the Smithsonian by the Patent Office adds an authentic note to the story of American machines.

406. This Kelly & Lamb indirect governor is dated 1865.

409

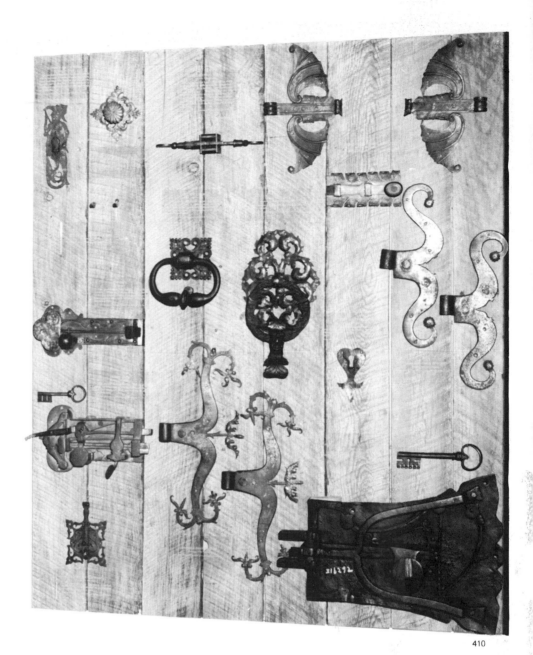

410

407. The structural materials of this reconstructed mid-nineteenth century machine shop are from a Harwinton, Connecticut, clock factory built in 1831 and razed in 1962. The shop is equipped with machine tools, hand tools, and accessories in use in 1855. On the left is a metal planing machine of about 1840, next to it an 1853 chain feed lathe and a screw cutting lathe of 1840 to 1850. On the right is a pulley lathe of about 1850.

408. The three nineteenth century woodworking tools shown mounted vertically are, left to right, a broadax for rough shaping of logs into beams, a chisel-edged broadax with the blade beveled on one side for finer hewing of logs, and a mortising ax or holax, used for trimming large mortises in framing beams. Across them is mounted an eighteenth century carpenter's hewing ax.

409. The chest key is thirteenth century English.

410. Locks, hinges, and other beautifully made door hardware are from the sixteenth, seventeenth and eighteenth centuries.

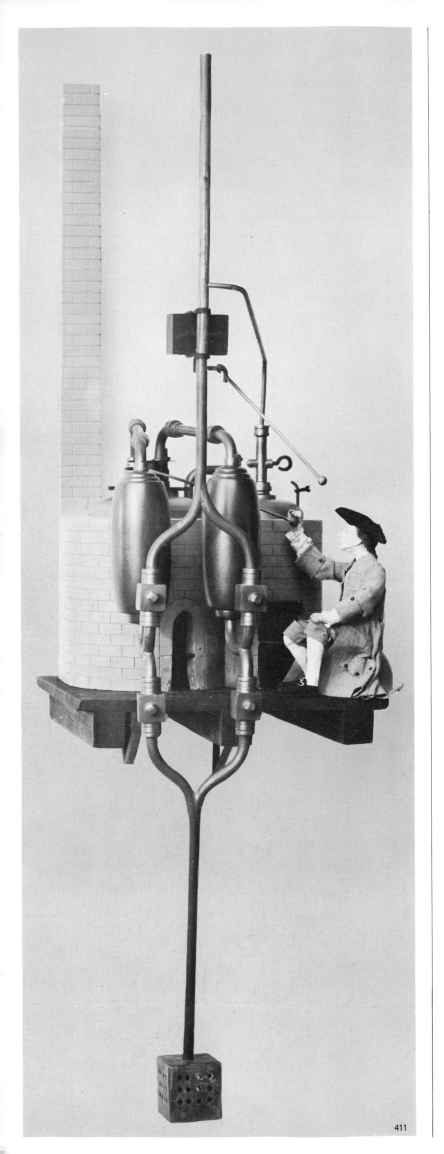

411

412

172

411. Because it is the first of its type for which positive records exist and the first to be manufactured commercially, the Thomas Savery steam-vacuum pump of 1698 may be considered the first practical steam engine. The model, with a scale portrait figure of the inventor, is based on an illustration in Savery's "The Miner's Friend." It was used to pump water from flooded mine shafts but was not permanently successful because the high boiler pressure required was greater than the boilers of the time could withstand and explosions were frequent.

412. Oliver Evans' high-pressure steam engine of 1804, shown in this model, was the first of its kind built in the United States. It was a "double-acting" engine that admitted steam alternately on both sides of the piston. A small portrait figure of the inventor gives scale to this model.

413. Thomas Masters patented this domestic refrigerator and ice cream maker in 1844. It used ice and various salts. The patent model is cut away to show the interior.

414. Engine and boiler by John Stevens, used in his first steamboat, 1804.

413

414

415

416

417

422

423

418

419

420

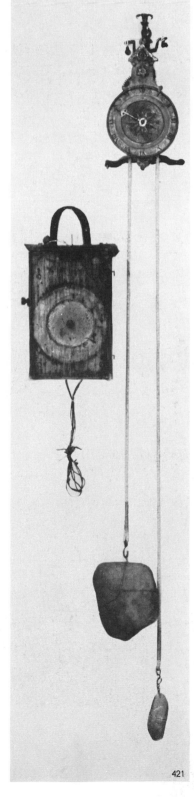

421

415. English eighteenth century. Made for the Turkish market, this alarm watch signed "Josh. Martineau London" strikes hours and quarter hours.
From the Frederick T. Proctor Collection.

416. Later wooden clocks include this clock, left, with the horizontal or Torrington movement, dated about 1820, made by Norris North. On the right is one of only a few spring-driven wooden-movement clocks known, made by Joseph Ives around 1825.

417. Civilized man has always endeavored to measure the passage of time. The sun dial is the simplest of his devices. Another early device is the sandglass, often attributed to an eighth century monk of Chartres.
On the left is a large sand clock. The sand in the four separate sandglasses falls at different speeds, indicating quarter hours.

418. Typical of later wooden clocks is one dated 1835.

419. This Eli Terry plain clock of about 1816 has a minimum of parts. The dial is painted on the glass face and the movement is open so the mechanism can easily be seen in operation.

420. In this Eli Terry design of about 1817 the escapement is the only visible part of the movement.

421. The first mechanical clock appeared somewhere in Europe in the late thirteenth or fourteenth century.
At the top is a Gothic clock from around 1500.
It is the earliest type of domestic clock.
Below it is an Austrian peasant clock typical of the middle seventeenth century.

422. One of the earliest typewriters produced was the Sholes, Glidden, Remington machine of 1873.
The carriage was weight driven and returned by foot pedal.

423. A nickel was dropped into this turn-of-the-century juke box, the coin operated gramaphone of 1897.
Some models contained several records, giving the customer a choice.

175

424

FARM MACHINERY

MANY VISITORS TO the Museum of History and Technology are surprised and delighted to recognize among the typical farm machinery of the nineteenth century machines with which they are familiar, for many are very similar to those used today. Along with the huge harvesters and tractors are early hand tools and plows. Patent models and models made from patent specification drawings help to tell the story of this important phase of American life.

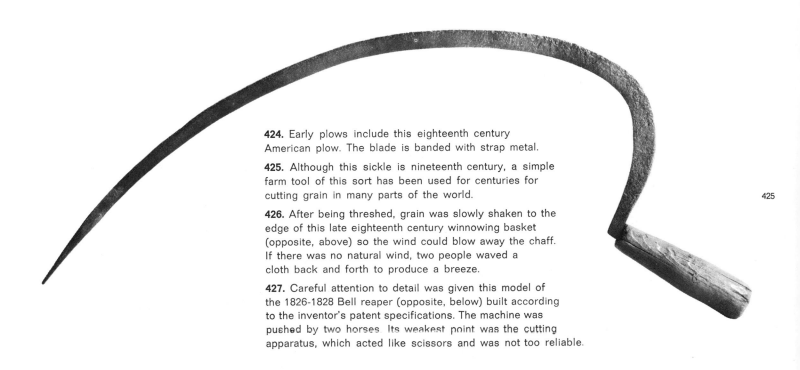

425

424. Early plows include this eighteenth century American plow. The blade is banded with strap metal.

425. Although this sickle is nineteenth century, a simple farm tool of this sort has been used for centuries for cutting grain in many parts of the world.

426. After being threshed, grain was slowly shaken to the edge of this late eighteenth century winnowing basket (opposite, above) so the wind could blow away the chaff. If there was no natural wind, two people waved a cloth back and forth to produce a breeze.

427. Careful attention to detail was given this model of the 1826-1828 Bell reaper (opposite, below) built according to the inventor's patent specifications. The machine was pushed by two horses. Its weakest point was the cutting apparatus, which acted like scissors and was not too reliable.

428. This model of the 1833 Hussey reaper was based on the patent specifications. A man rode one of the two horses to guide them while another man rode the machine to rake the cut grain off the platform.

429. This John Deere plow dated 1838 is one of three he made that year at Grand Detour, Illinois.

430. Shown is a transportable steam engine made by J. T. Case in 1869, which developed eight horsepower for driving threshers and sawmills by belts. The stack folded back for moving, bringing the driver's seat into position.

428

429

430

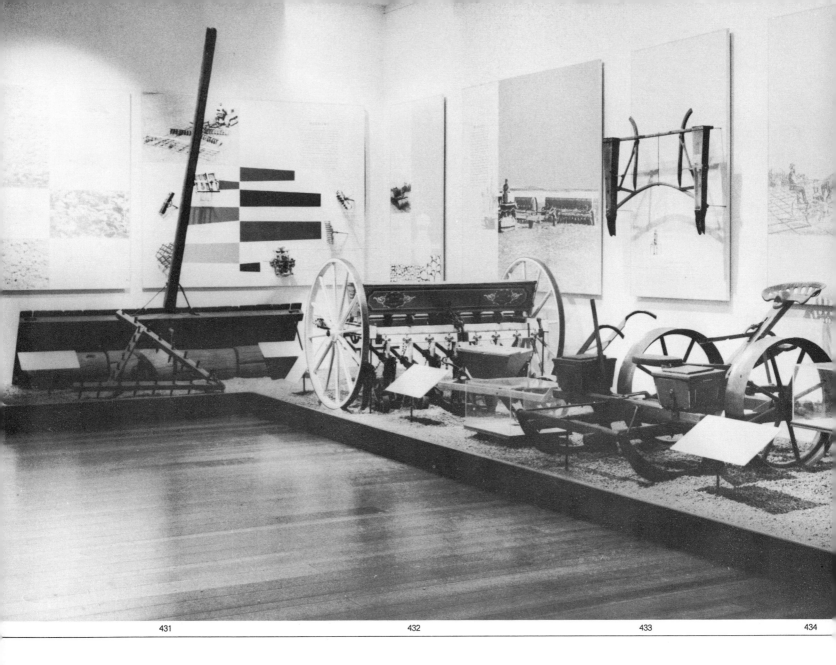

431   432   433   434

431. Typical nineteenth century farm machines include
the roller, left, made of sections of logs and drawn by oxen.
In front of it is an "A" harrow.

432. Next is a wheeled grain drill. Small seeds or grain
dropped through the tubes into the furrows.

433. Hanging on the wall, is a two-row hand planter
of about 1860. Advertisements for the machine claimed
that a man could plant as fast as he could walk.

434. The two-row horse-drawn planter has large iron wheels.

435. Hung on the wall is a hand-powered broadcast planter.

436. A cultivator.

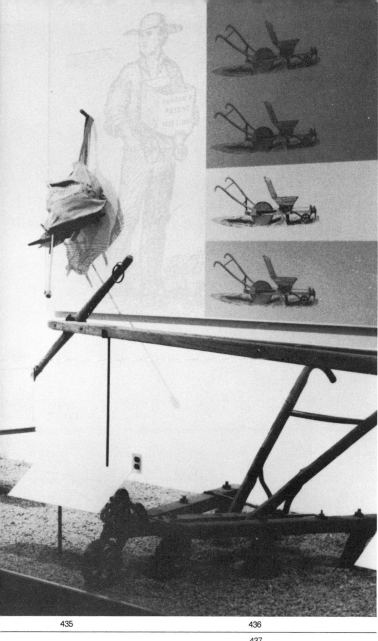

435

436

437

437. This vacuum pan is the original pan used in 1853 by Gail Borden for condensing milk. He was awarded a patent for the process in 1856.

T HE ECONOMIC BACKBONE of the United States is its industries. The tremendous growth of industry in the nineteenth century was a direct result of the abundant resources of coal, iron, oil, and lumber available. The production and refining of petroleum is an example of American industry itself while its end products supply the power for or are an important ingredient of many industrial processes.

Exhibits covering many of the major industries are planned for the Museum of History and Technology.

438. The Osgood dredging machine was patented in 1877.

439. Shown is the Wilson and Fox gas meter dated 1860.

440. Oil for kerosene production was shipped in pairs of wood tanks on flatcars. Called "Densmore cars," they carried 50 barrels or 2150 gallons. Model.

441. The three-high gray mill was first used for rolling steel rails.

442. William O. Crocker patented this hot-air furnace in 1875.

443. One important step forward in the production of iron and steel was this Kelly converter, used in 1861 and 1862 at the Cambria Iron Works, Johnstown, Pennsylvania, to make malleable iron from molten pig iron by blowing air through it.

444. On the left is a miner's cap carbide lamp of about 1920. The other miner's cap lamps burned lard or heavy oil and are turn-of-the-century lamps.

445 This coal puncher greatly advanced the technology of mining in 1888. The bit, not shown, was attached on the left.

446. The earliest of the heavy industries to start in the Colonies was the production of pig iron. Blast furnaces were built which turned out pigs of iron that were formed in a sand casting bed in front of the blast furnace. This pig iron is marked "Tubal 1753 Works" and is from the Spottswood furnace near Fredericksburg, Virginia.

441

INDUSTRIES

442

443

444

445

446

447

44

ELECTRICITY

F ROM THE "PHILOSOPHICAL TOYS" of the early nineteenth century to the electronic miracle of *Telestar* is but a mere century and a half, a very short span of time for a new way of life to become established and to dominate the civilized world. The invention and development of the electrical devices that twentieth century man takes for granted make a fascinating story told by the machines and patent models of the inventors.

449

450

447. Faraday's "Rotator" of 1821 was considered an amusing experimental toy in English scientific circles.
As shown by this model, the bar magnet in the center exerted a rotating force on the current in the wire.

448. A year later another "philosophical toy," Barlow's wheel, demonstrated that a horseshoe magnet exerted a rotating force on the current in the spokes.

449. In 1837, Thomas Davenport, a Brandon, Vermont, blacksmith, received the first American patent for an electric motor, shown by his patent model.

450. Charles G. Page submitted this patent model of his electric motor.

451. Alexander Graham Bell presented his tuned-reed telephone receiver to the Smithsonian Institution in 1908. It is probably the instrument Bell and his assistant used in 1876 in the first transmission of sound.

451

452

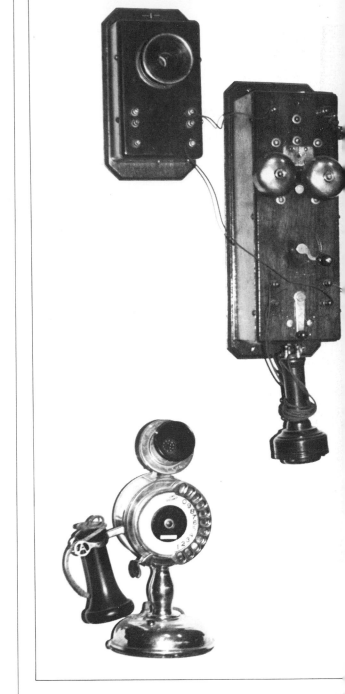

452. In April, 1877, Emile Berliner patented a telephone transmitter using loose metal contacts such as those in his 1877 "Soapbox" transmitter shown.

453. Bell recited the Hamlet soliloquy "To be or not to be . . ." into this receiver, which converted the sound into a varying electric current. The current was reconverted into speech by an iron-box receiver held by the Emperor Don Pedro of Brazil at the Philadelphia Centennial in 1876. The emperor exclaimed "My God, it talks!"

454. Early commercial telephones include the first commercial wall telephone, dated 1878, shown in the upper left; an 1885 wall set with improved Blake transmitter, right; and the Stowger telephone of 1905, lower left.

455. Pictured is a model made about 1890 of the 1876 Bell patent telephone transmitter. It was used to prove to the courts that the 1876 instruments would transmit sound under the proper conditions.

456. The experiments with vacuum radio tubes of the American inventor, Lee De Forest, laid the foundation for modern radio transmission and reception. The De Forest power tube is the prototype of all later power tubes and amplifiers. It was used as a generator for short distance radio telephone transmission.

453

457

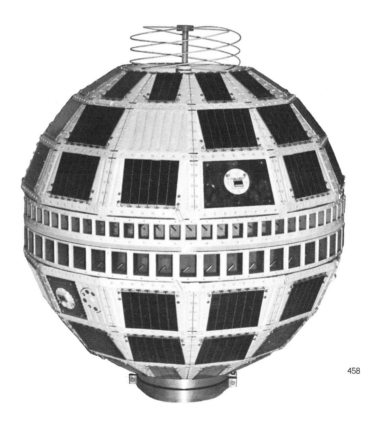

458

454

456

THE SMITHSONIAN INSTITUTION has a complete collection of communications satellites of the United States. Those on exhibit are not the ones put into orbit but were fully operating "standbys" ready to be launched in case of failure.

457. The *Courier* was launched in October, 1960, as a military experiment. It was activated by a complex code to prevent unauthorized stations from gaining access to it.

458. *"Telestar I"* was launched July, 1962, for the first time making it possible to transmit television signals reliably across the Atlantic.

187

RAILROADS

45

LOCOMOTIVES, BECAUSE of their size, are difficult to display in a museum, but because railroads played such an important part in the history of this country a few are shown in the Museum of History and Technology, even though the building had to be built around the largest of them. Along with the original engines, many of the historic and picturesque locomotives of the past are displayed in model form.

459. The drive wheel of the Pacific-type locomotive is seventy-three inches in diameter.

460. The original "Puffing Billy" of 1813-14 is in the Science Museum in London, England.

461. Colonel John Stevens built a railway on his New Jersey estate in 1825 to demonstrate the practicality of railroads and to arouse public interest.

462. Richard Trevithick's 1803 locomotive is generally considered to be the first steam locomotive. The original (shown in a scale model) hauled a ten-ton load on its initial run in a South Wales mine. The machine was a success but the mine's plateway was too weak to support it.

463. The water tube is from John Stevens' 1825 locomotive.

460

461

462

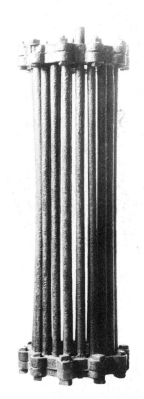

463

189

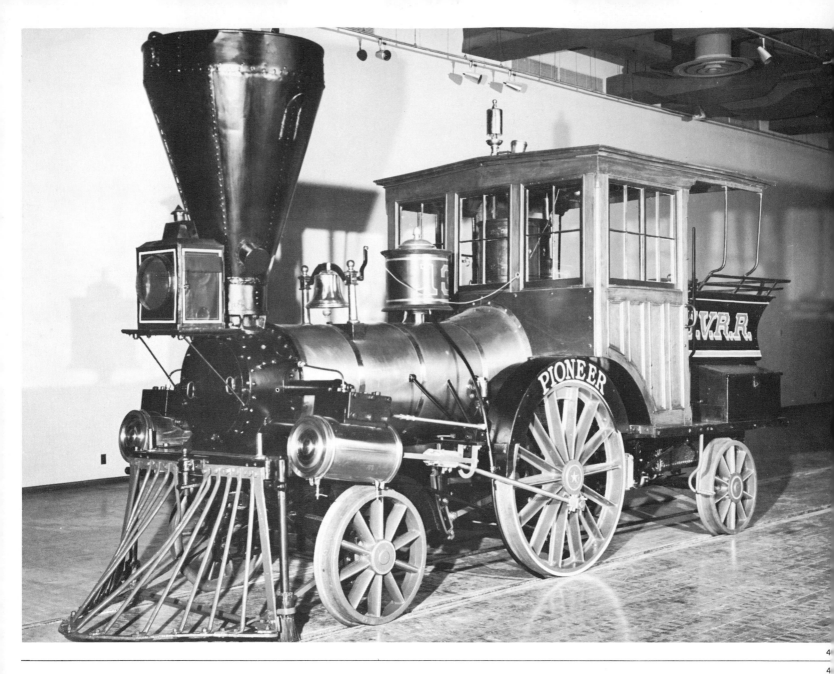

190

464, 465. Traveling at about forty miles per hour, the "Pioneer" locomotive of 1851 pulled three- or four-car passenger trains for the Cumberland Valley railroad in central Pennsylvania. The locomotive was damaged in 1862 when a Confederate raiding party led by General Stuart burned the company's railroad shops at Chambersburg, Pennsylvania. The "Pioneer" was repaired and continued in full service until 1880 and was retired in 1910. Shown is the interior of the engineer's cab.

466. The cable car grip is the center grip type of the kind still in use in San Francisco. It was tightened by pulling back on the lever. The steel jaws must be replaced each week.

467. The earliest of the distinctive standard type American locomotives, popular for fifty years, was the "Lancaster" of 1834. One outstanding feature was its swivel truck. The model is made to the scale ½ in. = 1 ft.

466

467

468. The "No. 1" of 1895 was the first electric locomotive on a main line. It was used on the B & O's Baltimore tunnel line.

469. The New York Central "No. 1173" of 1926 was the type used for passenger service operating out of New York City.

470. On the right in this view of Railroad Hall is the "Pacific" type locomotive of 1926. In the foreground is the "Pioneer" of 1851; behind it is the 1934 diesel engine that powered the "Pioneer Zephyr"; and in the rear the 1836 passenger coach of the Camden & Amboy Railway, capable of carrying forty-eight passengers.

471. The "DD-1" locomotive built for the Pennsylvania Railroad in 1910 was one of the most successful electric locomotives built.

468

469

470

471

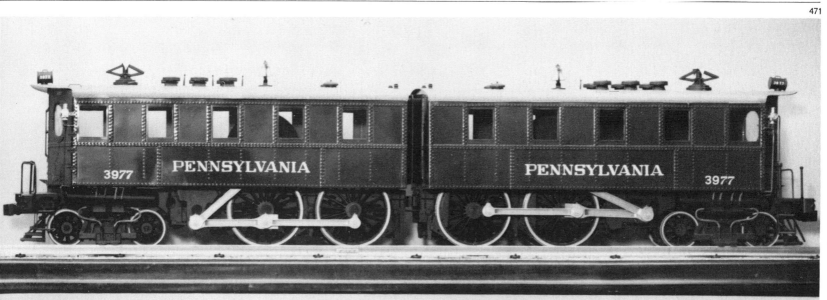

CIVIL ENGINEERING

472

EVEN MORE IMPOSSIBLE to exhibit than a railroad locomotive is the bridge that carries it over an obstacle or the tunnel that carries it under one. Yet the story of western man would not be complete without telling of the art of the civil engineer through the ages.

473

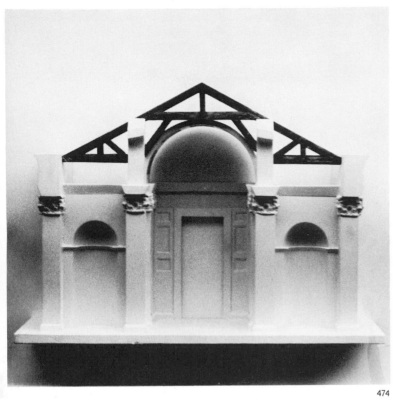

472. Shown is the center portion of a model of the Niagara Bridge built by Roebling in 1855. The 825-foot-long wire bridge carried a railway.

473. Roebling built an 825-foot railroad bridge over the Niagara River in 1885. Shown is a section of the bridge cable.

474. In the second century the Emperor Hadrian had a bronze truss installed to support the roof of the Pantheon in Rome. This apparent attempt at fireproofing is the earliest known structural use of metal.

475. The first underwater tunnel completed in North America was the St. Clair River Tunnel between Port Huron, Michigan, and Sarnia, Ontario, opened in 1890. With the digging of the tunnel, shown in the three-dimensional model, the railway systems of the United States and Canada were connected.

474

475

478

479

476. The first metal bridge was the Coalbrookdale bridge, a one hundred foot span over the Severn River in England. Built in 1779, the bridge is still in use.

477. This explanatory three-dimensional exhibit shows the use of compressed air rather than a shield to support the soft silt of the riverbed during the construction of Haskin's Hudson River Tunnel of 1879 to 1889 between New York and New Jersey. Shown is the Jersey City shaft of the tunnel. Wrought iron plating provided temporary support before the permanent brick lining was placed. At the left is a diagram showing how the air lock worked.

478. Part of the bridge that stood at Halcottsville, New York, from 1870 to 1948 is this end section of web plank from a Town truss.

479. Roebling is best remembered for his famous and beautiful Brooklyn Bridge in New York City, of which one pier is shown in construction in this model. This specimen of main cable from the Brooklyn Bridge is composed of 5282 individual wires.

480. By the year 1615 wrought iron was used in England to support a suspension foot bridge. The suspension bridge is an arch in reverse. John Finley invented the suspension bridge in its present form. His bridge over Jacob's Creek in southeast Pennsylvania was similar to a model shown in the hall. The sample chain is of the type used in 1807 to build the 130 foot Chain Bridge across the Potomac River above Washington, D.C.

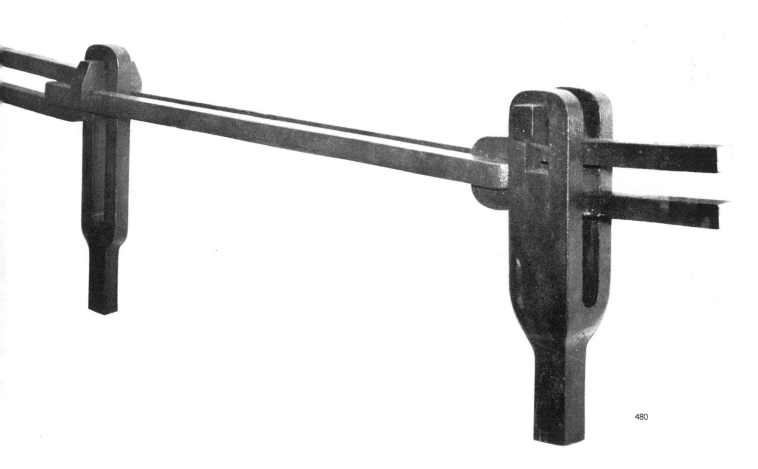

480

197

AUTOS AND COACHES

THAT GREAT INVENTION, the wheel, was soon put to work carrying loads or passengers. Thus in the pre-dawn of history the vehicle was born. Man or animal power was required to move these machines from place to place. Over the centuries many refinements were made, but basically vehicles remained much like this American Red River cart (481.) of the Civil War period until self-propelled vehicles were devised.

482. The interior of the Saltonstall coach was richly upholstered.

483. Henry Beckley built this farm wagon of 1860, from Bedford County, Pennsylvania.

484. Made famous by the Abbot-Downing Company of Concord, New Hampshire, the Concord Stagecoach of 1848 provided mail and passenger service to areas without access to railroads. Coaches of this type were in use for more than seventy-five years.

485. This Saltonstall family coach was built in 1851 by Thomas Goddard of Boston.

482

483

484

485

486

487

486. A light sleigh such as this Albany Cutter, also known as a swell-body cutter, usually was made to carry two passengers, but a less common four passenger version was built. This one was made in Newark, New Jersey, by Gilbert Vanderverken who, in 1849, established an omnibus service in Washington, D.C.

487. The inexpensive, easy-to-operate, fairly reliable Model T Ford established the automobile as the major vehicle of the century. This model is dated 1913.

488. A popular vehicle of its time was this 1918 Oldsmobile Model 37 touring car. Its selling price was $1185. The top could be let down and side curtains could be attached.

489. This Franklin Model 10C automobile was made in 1924.

490. This Columbia tandem is dated 1896. In 1897 Louis S. Clark built the Autocar 3-wheeler.

491. This patent model of a gasoline automobile was submitted by George B. Selden in 1879. He was granted a patent in 1895. Around 1906, and not in 1877 as is so often thought or implied by automotive historians, a full-sized version of this vehicle was built as an exhibit for the court while the famous Selden patent suit was underway. It was, however, powered by Selden's original engine built in the 1870's.

492. This 1869 velocipede, powered by steam, was built by Roper, a pioneer in the steam propelled vehicle field.

493. The electric truck was built in 1913 by the Commercial Company.

494. The Columbia Ordinary Light Roadster bicycle of 1888 was thought by many to be the best built light bicycle in the United States.

495. Considered by many the first American automobile, this machine built by Charles E. and J. Frank Duryea operated on the streets of Springfield, Massachusetts, in 1893. At that time it had friction drive. The present transmission was installed in 1894. It has a one cylinder, one stroke, four horse power water-cooled gasoline engine. Up and down movement of the tiller shifts gears to give two forward speeds and reverse.

488

489

490

491

492

493

494

495

KLOSTER-VEILSDORF
About 1765

LUDWIGSBURG
1760–70

HOCHST
About 1770
Trembleuse cup and saucer.

LUDWIGSBURG
1760–70

LUDWIGSBURG
1760–70

LUDWIGSBURG
About 1760
Tea set.

Gift of Pres. & Mrs. Dwight D. Eisenhower

18TH-CENTURY
GERMAN PORCELAIN

497

496. The eighteenth century German porcelain shown is from Ludwigsburg, except for the Trembleuse cup and saucer (upper right) which is Hockot.

497. The Faience plate is French.

CERAMICS

PRIMITIVE PEOPLES in all parts of the world made some sort of fired clay container. Many early civilizations developed the craft to a fine art.

The Egyptians used brilliant glazes which were applied before the clay vessel was fired or applied before a second firing. All parts of the Roman empire knew something of pottery work.

The greatest ceramics workers were the Chinese. Their superb white translucent porcelain became known as *china* around the world.

Hand painted decoration of ceramic pieces gave way to the technique of decoration by machine printing, developed by the English.

Many types of native American ceramic ware were produced, from the simple Colonial ware to the elaborate creations of the late nineteenth century.

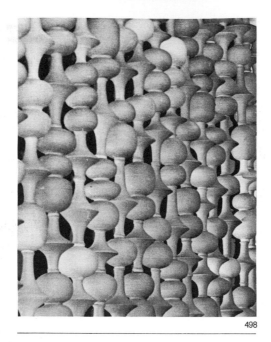

498

500

499

501

502

498. A variety of shapes combine to make a decorative ceramic screen dividing the various sections of the exhibition hall.

499. Much Staffordshire pottery was made for export to the United States and decorated with typical American scenes such as this Glens Falls, New York, pitcher.

500. The porcelain figurines are late nineteenth century Meissen.

501. The teapot of English stoneware is from the period 1790 to 1820.

502. "Mocha" ware was introduced before 1800 and was made for nearly a hundred years.

503. These examples of pâte-sur-pâte porcelain were produced at the Minton factory at Stoke-on-Trent, England, from 1870 to 1904.

PÂTE-SUR-PÂTE PORCELAIN

504

506

504. Worcester porcelain of the Dr. Wall period, 1751 to 1783, includes the handsome tea set and platter.

505. Worcester porcelain of the period 1792 to 1813 includes this piece with bat-printed decoration of the Barr, Flight, and Barr period.

506. The elaborately decorated porcelains are German eighteenth century Meissen.

505

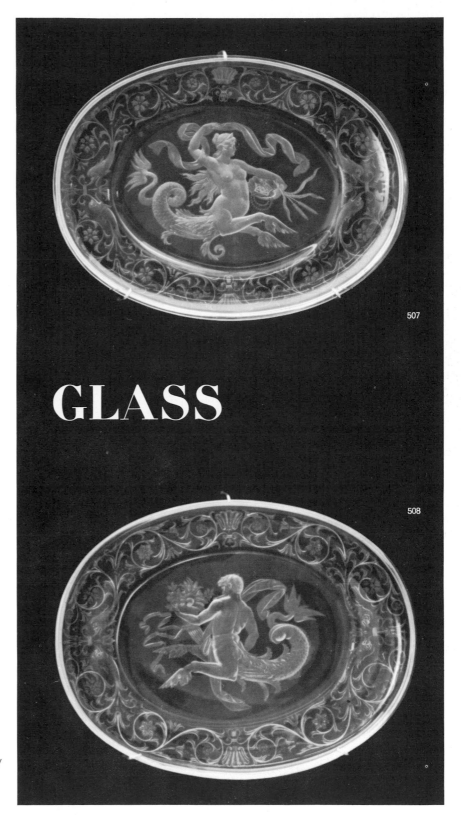

507, 508. The two engraved plates are from the Lobmyer factory in Vienna and are of exceptional quality. At the top is a Meerweibschale plate; at the bottom a Tritonschale plate, both about 1873.

GLASS

SINCE THE TIME of the pharaohs, glass has been fashioned into useful objects that have also been works of art, perhaps because of the inspiration gained from the nature of the raw material itself. American-made glass has always been treasured and has taken its place with the finest in the world.

509

509. The Boston and Sandwich Company of Sandwich, Massachusetts, which produced these candlesticks, was established in 1825 and produced free blown and mold blown pieces. It closed January 1, 1888.

510. Venetian glass was made as early as the eleventh century A.D. The Venetian glassmakers guild was established as early as the thirteenth century A.D., but none of the thirteenth or fourteenth century glass is known to exist today.

At the top are two vases and a ewer.
At the bottom are bowls and plates of latticinio and vitro di trina, a method of fabricating glassware with decorative threads of opaque white or colored glass.

511, 512. These ancient pieces of glass acquired their iridescence from the reaction on the glass of the earth in which they had lain buried for centuries.

513. Art glass of the United States includes the early twentieth century pitcher and goblet made by the Union Glass Company of Somerville, Massachusetts.

VENETIAN GLASS

Venetian craftsmen revived and further developed many ancient Roman techniques. The Venetian names for these early glass types were:

Millefiori—glass tesserae (bits of glass) fused together in a mosaic-type design or embedded in clear glass.

Latticino and *vitro-di-trina*—both processes in which threads of opaque white or colored glass were fabricated into decorations.

511

512

513

514

515

516

514. This bowl is of Sandwich lacy glass and is dated 1830.

515. Selected from the Smithsonian's collection of paperweights are Gilliand paperweights made in the United States in the mid-nineteenth century.

516. Steuben glass is one of the finest kinds of glass produced in America. The company was founded in 1903 by Frederick Carder. During World War I it was purchased by Corning Glass Works and was operated as the Steuben Division until 1932 when it became Steuben Glass, Inc. Since 1932 Carder has been art director of the Corning Glass Works. Steuben glass, such as this bird from the period 1903 to 1932, is famous for its purity and brilliance.

517. Besides stained glass for which he is so famous, Louis Tiffany produced art glass, two pieces of which are shown here.

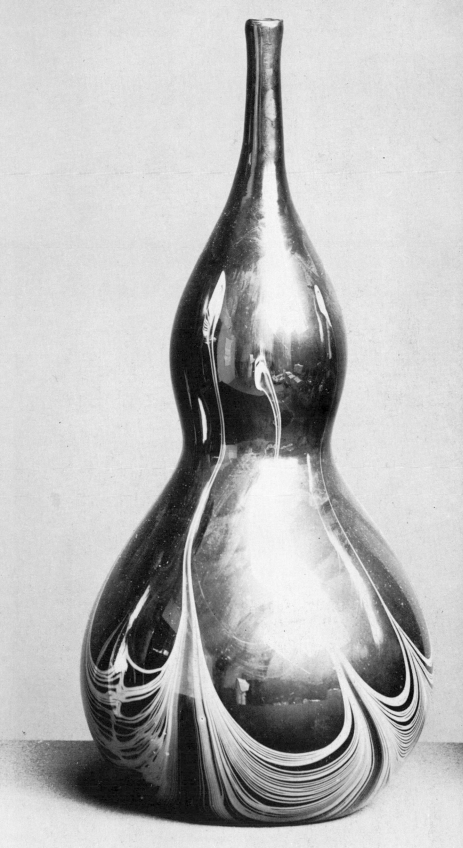

211

hostes nrī. Nesciant et ignorent donec
veniam⁹ in mediū eoꝝ ⁊ interficiam⁹
eos:et cessare faciamus opus. Factū
est aūt venientibꝫ iudeis ꝗ habitabāt
iuxta eos ⁊ dicentibꝫ nobis per decem
vices ex omnibus locis quibus vene-
rant ad nos:statui in loco post muꝝ
per circuitū ipsm in ordine cū gladijs
suis et lanceis et arcubus. Et perspexi
atꝗ surrexi · et aio ad optimates et
magistratus·et ad reliquā parte vul-
gi. Nolite timere a facie eoꝝ. Domini
magni · ⁊ terribilis mementote : et pu-
gnate pro fratribus vrīs·filijs vrīs·⁊
filiabꝫ vrīs·et vxoribꝫ vrīs·et domnibꝫ
vrīs. Factū est aūt cū audissent inimi-
ci nrī nūciatū esse nobis:dissipauit deus cōsiliū eoꝝ. Et reuersi sum⁹ omnes
ad muros: unusquisꝗ ad opus suū.
Et factū est a die illa : media pars iu-
uenum eoꝝ faciebat opus·et media
parata erat ad bellū:et lancee·⁊ scuta·
et arcus·⁊ lorice:⁊ principes post eos
in omni domo iuda edificantiū mu-
ros:et portantiū onera et imponentū.
Una manu sua faciebat opus : et al-
tera tenebat gladiū. Edificantiū eni
unusquisꝗ gladio erat accinctus re-
nes. Et edificabat ⁊ clangebat bucina
iuxta me. Et dixi ad optimates et ad
magistratus:⁊ ad reliquā parte vul-
gi. Opus grande est et latū:et nos sepe-
rati sumus in muro procul alter ab
altero. In loco quocunꝗ audieritis
clangorem tube:illuc occurrite ad nos.
Deus noster pugnabit pro nobis:et
nos ipi faciam⁹ op⁹. Et media pars
nrm teneat lanceas·ab ascensu aurore
donec egrediatur astra. In tpe quoqꝫ
illo dixi ppło. Unusquisꝗ cum puero
suo maneat i medio ihrlm:et sint uo-
bis vices per nocte et die ad operādū.

Ego aūt et fratres mei et pueri mei · et
custodes ꝗ erant post me:nō deponeba-
mus vestimēta nrā. Unusquisꝗ tan-
tū nudabatur ad baptismum.

Et factus est clamor ppłi et vxorū
eius magnus:aduersus fratres
suos iudeos. Et erāt qui dicerent. Filij
nostri et filie nostre multe sunt nimis.
Accipiam⁹ pro pcio eoꝝ frumentū:et
comedamus ⁊ uiuam⁹. Et erāt ꝗ dicerent. Agros nros ⁊ vineas et domos
nras opponam⁹:et accipiam⁹ frumē-
tum in fame. Et alij dicebat. Mutuo
sumam⁹ pecunias in tributa regis:de-
musꝗ agros nros ⁊ vineas. Et nūc
sicut carnes fratꝝ nostroꝝ sic carnes
nre sunt:⁊ sicut filij eoꝝ ita et filij nrī.
Ecce nos subiugam⁹ filios nros et fi-
lias nras in seruitutem:⁊ de filiabus
nostris sunt famule·nec habem⁹ unde
possint redimi : et agros nostros ⁊ vineas nras alij possidet. Et irat⁹ sum
nimis : cū audissem clamore eoꝝ secu-
dū in verba hec. Cogitauitꝗ cor meū.
Et increpui optimates ⁊ magistrat⁹:
⁊ dixi eis. Usurasne singuli a fratribꝫ
vestris exigitis? Et congregaui adūlu
eos contionem magnam : et dixi eis.
Nos ut scitis redemim⁹ fratres nros
iudeos qui venditi fuerāt gentibus se-
cundū possibilitate nostrā. Et vos igi-
tur vendite fratres nros:et redimem⁹
eos? Et siluerūt:nec inuenerut qd re-
spōderet. Dixiꝗ ad eos. Nō est bona
res quā facitis. Quare nō in timore
dei nostri ambulatis:ne exprobretur
nobis agentibus inimicis nrīs? Et
ego ⁊ fratres mei et pueri mei comoda-
uimus plurimis pecuniā ⁊ frumentū.
Non repetamus in comune istud. Es
alienū cocedamus:quod debetur nobis. Reddite eis hodie agros suos:et

519

520

GRAPHIC ARTS AND PHOTOGRAPHY

RAPHIC ARTS PROCESSES include those which result in a work of art and those by which a drawing or text is reproduced. Many of the great masters turned their hands to the creation of etchings, dry points, and lithographs now prized by the great museums.

The Gutenberg Bible was printed with movable metal type which was cast from a matrix, the earliest known use of this technique which is still in use today.

Wood engraving was a major means of producing an illustration for publication in the nineteenth century. Magazines such as *Frank Leslie's Illustrated Weekly* relied on engravings such as the one showing President Grant and the Emperor of Brazil starting the Corliss Engine at the Centennial Exhibition in Philadelphia.

With the perfection of photographic techniques the graphic arts processes underwent a change. Now the production of type itself relies heavily on the camera. As with etching and lithography, photography can be a tool for reproducing graphics or can be an art in itself.

518. The earliest known book printed with movable type is the Gutenberg Bible, printed about 1455. The page shown contains the third and fourth chapters of the 2 Esdras, known in the King James version as the Book of Nehemiah.

519. One of the famous etchings shown at the Columbia Exposition was *Christ Preaching* by Rembrandt (1606–1669), dated about 1650.

520. President Grant and the Emperor of Brazil starting the Corliss Engine at the Centennial Exhibition in Philadelphia, 1876.

521. Lithography is a method of printing using a porous stone such as the one shown. Only one type of stone is adaptable to the process, limestone from the Solenhofen quarries in Bavaria, Germany. The porous stone is sensitive to, and capable of absorbing, both water and grease. Metal plates, processed to have these properties, have entirely replaced stone for industrial printing. The drawing on the stone is by Russell T. Limbach, entitled *Summer*.

521

213

522

523
524

522. Benjamin Franklin worked at this press as a journeyman printer at the Watts' Printing House in London in 1726.

523. Adam Ramage became the best known early manufacturer of printing presses in the United States. His press, made of wood and iron, is dated around 1820.

524. The United States' first important contribution to printing was the lever press. Invented in 1813, the Columbian press of this type is dated 1865.

525. Sir Charles Wheatstone of England first demonstrated the principle of stereoptics in 1832. The first stereo photographs were taken in 1841 by Henry Collen. Shown is a typical stereoptican.

526. This daguerreotype camera was used around 1850.

527. George Eastman popularized photography when the first Kodak was made available in 1888. It was the first camera to use the roll film arrangement. Costing twenty-five dollars, it took one hundred pictures before being returned to the factory for processing and reloading for the price of ten dollars.

528. In 1861 James Maxwell devised a system of projecting color separation pictures. Frederic Eugene Ives, of Philadelphia, patented his Ives Lantern Kromshop in 1890, which projected color separation pictures.

529. Pictures were first projected on a screen in 1656 by the Dutch physicist Huygens, using an instrument basically similar to the magic lantern, a direct ancestor of the modern motion picture projector.

530. After successfully recording sound and adding motion to photography, Edison proceeded to combine the two. His picture-sound synchronizer, *circa* 1908, synchronized a phonograph record and film projection.

531. Although there is a similar Edison movie camera in the collection, the one shown is operated manually.

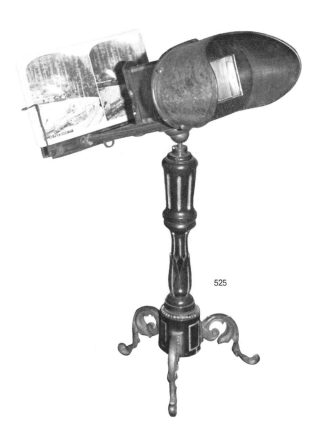

525

526

529

527

530

528

531

EDISON MOTION PICTURE CAMERA

532

533

ANYONE LOOKING FOR sunken treasure should search the Caribbean, for that romantic sea holds in her depths many sunken ships of the seventeenth and later centuries whose positions are known from records of the time. Hundreds of others went down from natural or man-made causes with no hint remaining as to their whereabouts. But no small task confronts the treasure seeker, for underwater salvage is expensive and dangerous.

The Smithsonian Institution has participated in several diving expeditions which, along with gold and silver, have yielded ordinary objects giving valuable clues to life in times long past.

UNDERWATER EXPLORATION

532. The Smithsonian Institution has participated in several diving expeditions which, along with gold and silver, have yielded ordinary objects giving valuable clues to life in times long past.

533. Sections of a certain weight called cobs were often cut from flat silver bars, stamped with a crest, and used for money. Shown are two eight-real cobs, two four-real cobs and the small half-real cob found off one of the Florida Keys where a whole fleet was sunk in 1715. An example of an eight-real piece is the round coin dated 1817.

534. The section of gold chain is from the Spanish vessel *San Antonio* lost off Bermuda in 1621. The crosses were recovered from the Spanish ship *El Mantancero* lost off Yucatán in 1740. One cross is unpolished.

535. The cannon barrel is shown encrusted with barnacles and corals just as it was found on board the Spanish ship *Genovese* sunk off Jamaica in 1628.

536. The three-pronged iron object was probably an incendiary hand projectile. Wrapped with oil soaked cloth and set on fire, it was thrown at the sail or powder supply of the ship. The one shown is from a ship sunk in 1733.

537. Lost in 1702 off the coast of Ceylon this clump of silver rupees retains the shape of the bag which held them.

534

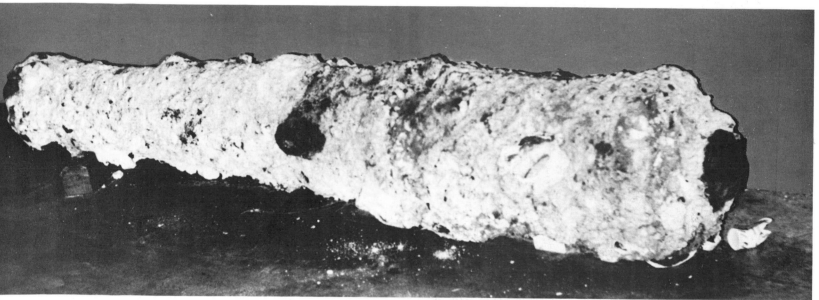

535

536

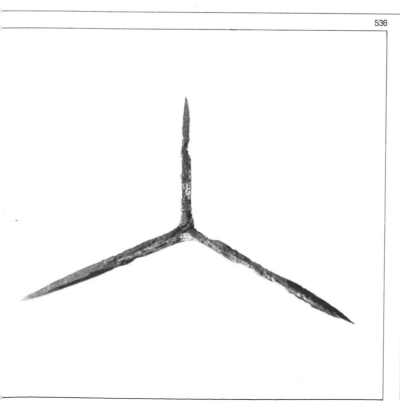

537

538

NUMISMATICS

MONEY IS OF GREAT interest to every one, but few people know much of its history. Yet almost every major event in the historical development of our civilization can be symbolized by a coin. From the "staters" of Lydia and Corinth, through the coins of Greece, Rome, Byzantium, the Dark Ages, and climaxing with the early Colonial, Confederate, and modern United States currency, coins of bronze, copper, silver, and gold, and the squares of paper which symbolize them, tell the complete history of Western Man.

538. The *Libral As* was a cast bronze coin of ancient Rome of 222 B.C.

539. In the last years of the Roman Republic, coins which once bore portraits only of gods and great ancestors began to promote the fame of Roman emperors. On the left is a typical *aureus* dated 42 B.C.; on the right the coin bears a likeness of Julius Caesar.

540. The penny has derived from the denier, left, issued by Charlemagne at the time of his money reform in 781. The penny and shilling-pound relationship, of which the silver penny was the basis, is still used in England. The *light denier* was issued before the 781 reform.

541. The two Byzantine coins were brought out by Basil II, 976 to 1025, on the left; Romanus III, 1028 to 1034; and on the right, Constantine X, 1059 to 1067.

542. Because they bore the image of Pegasus, the staters of Corinth of 625 B.C. were called *poloi* or "colts." Shown by replicas.

543. Hard money was scarce in the New World. One of the few coins brought by settlers was the English *unite* of 1625. On the right is a 1652 ten shilling gold piece.

539

540

541

542

543

545

544

546

BOHEMIA

547

548

549

550

551

552

553

554

555

556

557

558

559

560

544. The English crown was one of the major foreign coins circulating in the newly independent United States.

545. The *augustalia* of Frederick II of Hohenstaufen, 1198 to 1250, was the first major gold coin of the Middle Ages.

546. In 1518 the Counts of Schlick began minting silver from their mines in *Joachimstaler* and later *taler*. From this coin the Dutch *daler* and the American *dollar* were derived.

547. Spurred by the wealth of his silver mines, the Archduke Sigismond of Tyrol struck the first dollar-sized coin in 1486. The coin equaled in value the gold *gulden*.

548. The Reformation inspired this Nuremberg box medal with painted medallions by P.P. Werner, 1730.

549, 550. The first attempt at national currency was the Continental dollar struck in Philadelphia or Lancaster, Pennsylvania, by the Continental Congress in 1776.

551, 552, 553, 554. The earliest United States copper coins issued by the mint were the chain type cent and the half cent of 1793. Both sides of the coins are shown.

555, 556. The Mormons of Utah issued their own coins.

557, 558. *Hard Times Tokens* were so named because of their use in replacing scarce coinage during intermittently "hard times" from 1833 to 1842.

559, 560. Although gold was horded during the Civil War, in the North gold coins were available at a premium. The "Gold Room" in New York became the scene of regularly quoted gold prices. National banks were organized at this time as a replacement for the often unreliable state banks. Shown are the two sides of an 1864 gold double eagle.

221

561. The artist's plastilene model is for the obverse of the half dollar issued in commemoration of President Kennedy. The first of these fifty-cent pieces were struck at Philadelphia and Denver on February 11, 1964.

562. Massachusetts issued the first colonial paper money in 1690 to pay a debt incurred by an unsuccessful expedition against Canada.

563. Continental paper money was issued in 1775 but soon depreciated greatly, giving rise to the phrase "not worth a Continental." In 1790 Congress redeemed this currency at a ratio of 100 to 1. The United States of North America issued this forty-dollar note on January 14, 1779, with the Spanish milled dollar as the unit of value.

564. The states issued paper money similar to Continental currency, such as this Rhode Island six shilling note of 1767 to 1786.

565. By 1857 more than half the paper money in circulation was fraudulant. When 5,100 banks collapsed that year, their notes were called *broken bank bills.*

566. Lacking adequate taxation, the Confederate Government issued large amounts of paper money which depreciated rapidly. By the end of the war a billion dollars worth was in circulation.

567. The scarcity of coins of small denominations during the Civil War brought many kinds of emergency and substitute money into circulation. Shown are examples of cardboard currency.

568. Many beautiful contemporary medals are being designed. "The Samaritan" is by Francesco Giannone from Italy.

562

563

561

564

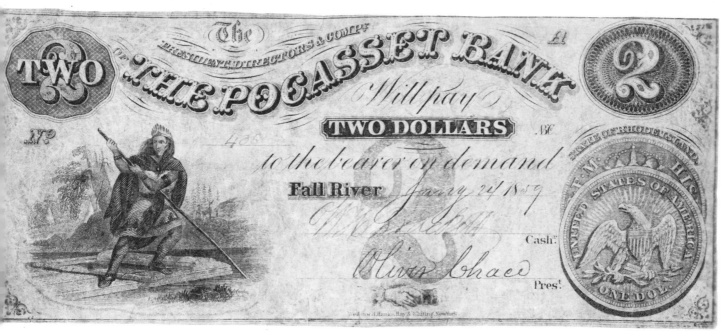

565

566

567

568

PHILATELY AND POSTAL HISTORY

THE SMITHSONIAN'S PHILATELIC collection contains millions of specimens of stamps of all kinds, ages, and nationalities. It is growing all the time as more stamps are issued by countries around the world. The Smithsonian receives three of each stamp design issued by the United States and is given new issues by many foreign countries.

A choice selection of stamps and associated items of special interest has been assembled to tell the history of postal service from an ancient letter written in cuneiform script dated around 2500 B.C. to the present day.

For the avid philatelist a systematic arrangement of display cases makes available for study more than three hundred thousand stamps.

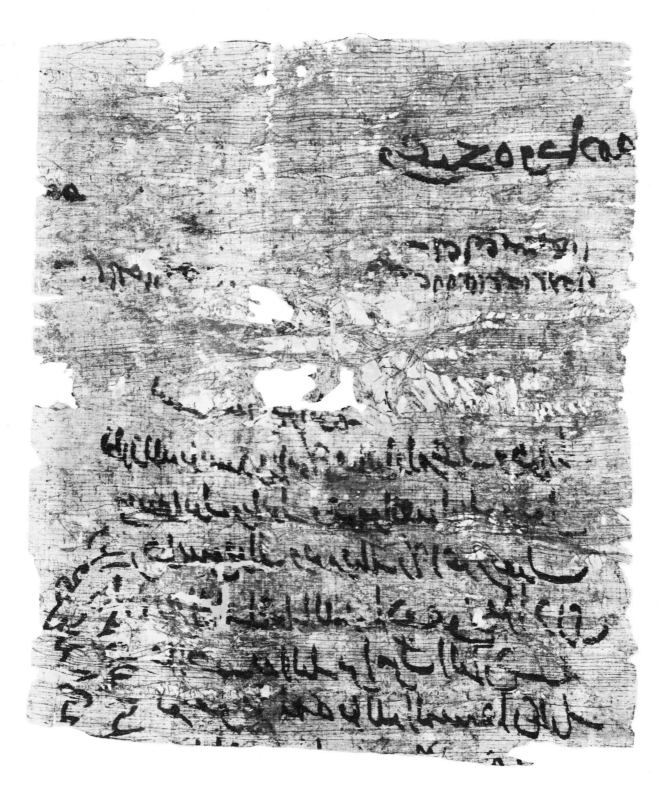

570

569. Used on country carrier routes, this rural mail wagon, shown by the model, offered registry and money-order services as well as delivering and collecting mail.

570. Egypt had courier service by 2000 B.C. and courier-relay stations by 1900 B.C. Two hundred years later horsemen had replaced foot runners. Letters on papyrus were written in hieratics, a simplified form of hieroglyphics.

225

571

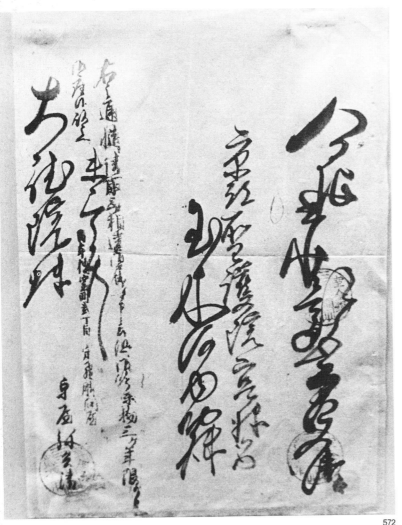

572

571. The Sumerians of the Mesopotamian area had what might be called the earliest postal service in 2500 B.C. Messages were written on clay tablets in cuneiform script. The two tablets shown are dated between 2500 and 2150 B.C.

572. Receipt for mail, Japanese, before 1871.

573. Early United States revenue stamps were used on commodities and documents to show that a tax had been paid. The revenue stamp proof shown was used from 1869 to 1871 on cigars.

574. This dead letter record of 1777-1788 was used to list undelivered valuable mail until just before the Post Office Department was reorganized under the Constitution.

575. The only known surviving piece of mail on the first mail-carrying flight authorized by a United States postmaster, was carried by John Wise on the balloon *Jupiter*, August 17, 1859, from Lafayette to Crawfordsville, Indiana.

576. The three stamps with inverted vignettes, issued in 1901, are very rare.

577. This letter, signed by the airship's commanding officer, was carried in 1929 by the United States Navy dirigible *Los Angeles* from Lakehurst, New Jersey, and dropped by message parachute over Orlando, Florida.

578. This letter was mailed in 1857 by pioneer balloonist John Wise.

579. On September 19, 1864, trans-Mississippi express service via Brandon, Mississippi, was given this letter from Montgomery, Alabama, to Galveston, Texas. The forty cents postage was prepaid by four ten cent stamps (1863 issue) —one pair and two single stamps.

580. Shown is President Roosevelt's original sketch for the 1934 Mother's Day stamp.

573

AMERICAN AIR MAIL SOCIETY
HARRY A. TRUBY, PRESIDENT
NEW KENSINGTON, PA.

DROPPED IN MESSAGE PARACHUTE
OVER ORLANDO, FLORIDA.

VIA
U.S. NAVY DIRIGIBLE LOS ANGELES
LAKEHURST,-U.S. ORLANDO, FLA.
JAN. 10, 1929.

C.E. Rosendahl

AMERICAN AIR MAIL SOCIETY
604-RIDGE AVENUE
NEW KENSINGTON, PENN.

577

Balloon Mail.
Prof Wise will take a Balloon mail from this city to-morrow. All persons who wish to send letters to the seaboard, will place them in the Post Office before twelve o'clock to-morrow, properly stamped, and directed "via Balloon."

Wm Markoe Esq
St Paul
M.T.

578

Lafayette, August 16

Dear Sir

Thinking you would be pleased to hear of my improved health I embrace the opportunity of sending you a line in this new and novel way of sending letters in a balloon.

Prof. Wise leaves the City of Lafayette this day at half past three in his balloon Jupiter and expects to land in Philadelphia or N York.

Love to all your affectionate friend
Mary A Will

N. H. Munn

575

576

579

580

581

585

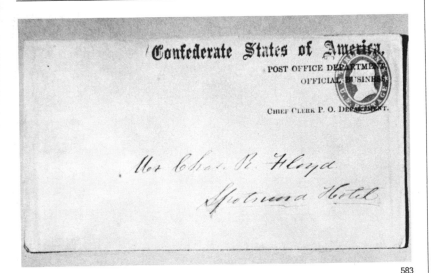

582

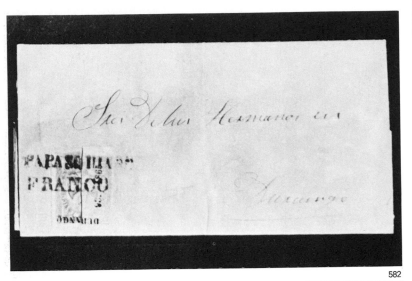

583

584

581. Illustrated envelopes became popular in the 1850's. Shown is a wartime camp scene.

582. Bisected stamp. Mexico, 1865. The government authorized the cutting of stamps to obtain half denominations.

583. Dated 1861 to 1865, the Confederate Post Office overprint appears on this old United States envelope, used for sending official postage free.

584. "Crash covers," such as this letter dated 1945, were mail salvaged from air disasters and forwarded with explanatory markings.

585. The heat of the flames of the great Chicago fire in October, 1871, caused this packet of stamps to stick together.

586. This letter bearing the official postmark depicting the Napoleonic eagle traveled from Cesclans to the commissioner of police in Tolmezzo, Italy, in 1812.

587. This 1779 letter shows the Washington city circular postmark. The rate was twenty cents per sheet for 300 to 500 miles.

588. Enterprising individuals carried mail between mining camps and the San Francisco Post Office. The handstamp "Noisy Carriers Mail" is the mark of Charles Kimball's local service on a ten cent stamped envelope mailed from San Francisco to West Cambridge, Massachusetts, in 1855.

589. This 1840 prepaid letter sheet was privately printed by J. N. Buchanan before government stamps or stationery became available in Great Britain.

590. In 1854, before the international rate reform, postage from England to the United States was one shilling per half ounce, here prepaid with a pair of embossed stamps issued in 1847 without perforations. After 1875, the rate was two-and-a-half pence per half ounce.

591. The Mulready one-penny letter sheet was the world's first prepaid, illustrated government postal stationery. William Mulready created allegoric designs depicting the benefits of Britain's postal reform,.

592. The world's first adhesive postage stamp dated 1840 pictures Queen Victoria. This stamp was canceled at Bridge of Eaton, England, with a red Maltese cross.

593. This letter was recovered after flight in 1949 in a V-2 rocket launched at White Sands Proving Grounds, Las Cruces, New Mexico.

228

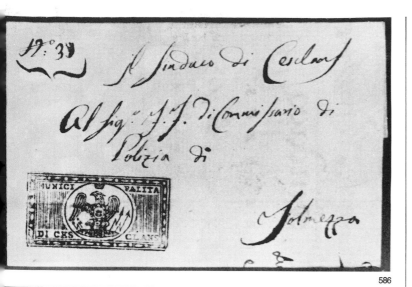

586

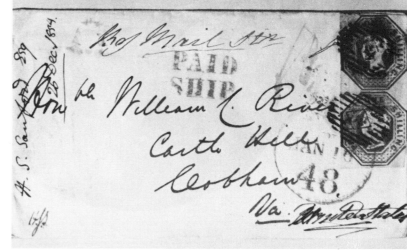

590

587

591

588

589

592

593

GOWNS OF THE FIRST LADIES

594. This silver snuffbox was a souvenir of the Dolley Madison breakfast in Washington in 1912 at which the First Ladies collection was born.

595. Carved with medallions of Presidents Washington and Jackson and General Lafayette, this comb was a presentation piece to President Jackson, who gave it to his niece, Emily Donelson.

596. Mrs. Washington made the satin drawstring bag from her own dresses combined with a piece of her husband's Continental Army uniform, embroidered in old style script across the front.

594

AT A DOLLEY MADISON breakfast held in 1921 in Washington, D.C., one of the most widely known collections of costumes was born. At that breakfast Mrs. William Howard Taft, a former First Lady, promised to present her 1912 inaugural gown to the Smithsonian Institution. The descendants of five other Presidents joined her in establishing a nucleus around which the now complete collection has been built.

Contrary to popular belief, not all the ladies represented were wives of Presidents and not all the gowns were inaugural gowns. When the President was a widower or a bachelor, his daughter or a close relative served as hostess for the Administration. In a few cases the health of the First Lady prohibited her carrying on the strenuous affairs of official life and a relative or family friend served as hostess in her stead. Only gowns worn by actual White House hostesses are in the collection.

Many inaugurations were held without elaborate festivities. Thus there is no inaugural ball gown available for some of the early First Ladies.

The Exhibition of Gowns of the First Ladies includes china, costume accessories, and mementos of many of the Presidents and their wives, as well as eight beautiful authentic room settings which serve as backgrounds for the gowned mannequins.

Many of the furnishings, draperies, carpets, moldings, mantles, and lighting fixtures came to the Smithsonian when the White House was refurbished or structural changes were made. These authentic items have been completed, or duplicated where necessary, to provide an accurate replica of a room in the White House (or Executive Mansion before the White House was built). The oval Blue Room is shown as it appeared in two different periods of 1869 to 1891 and 1893 to 1921.

The East Room, the setting for the most recent First Ladies, is spacious enough to display inaugural gowns of another fifty years.

596

597. Typical of the "sacque" period is Elizabeth Kortright Monroe's gown, left. The fabric of the dress is an unusually beautiful deep-cream taffeta brocaded in large bunches of deep red roses. The turban headdress was the most popular of the period. On state occasions Mrs. Monroe wore the topaz necklace purchased by President Monroe when he was Minister to France.

In the center is Marie Monroe Gouverneur, first daughter of a president to be married in the White House. Her pale blue silk gown in the late Empire style was imported from France in 1824.

Bell-shaped skirts that stood out from the figure had become popular by the time Louisa Catherine Adams, right, became first lady. Her dress is made of white net with silver braid.

The dessert service of which this plate is a piece was used by President James Monroe. It was made in France by Dagoty. On the border are five vignettes depicting commerce, agriculture, art, science, and warfare. In the center are the arms of the United States.

598. The Blue Room at the turn of the century had been decorated in robin's egg blue with elegant gold furniture. From left to right are Frances Folsom Cleveland, Ida Saxton McKinley, Edith Kermit Carow Roosevelt, Helen Herron Taft, Ellen Axson Wilson, and President Wilson's second wife, Edith Bolling Wilson. The first Mrs. Wilson wears a gown of white brocaded velvet in a rose design with the fashionable

hobble skirt, slashed far up the left side to reveal a lace and satin underskirt. The train of the underskirt ends in a point. Ropes of large pearls are attached.

599. Mrs. Washington, Mrs. John Adams, and Martha Jefferson Randolph, daughter of Thomas Jefferson, are seen in the drawing room of the Philadelphia Presidential Mansion.

Martha Washington wears a gown of salmon pink hand-painted faille, Mechlin lace shawl, lace mitts, and lace "mobcap" which she usually wore to all social functions. The First Lady herself made the brown satin bag she holds. The name "Mrs. Washington" is embroidered across the front of the bag.

Abigail Smith Adams wears a simple daytime dress of heavy blue Canton crepe. A Mechlin lace fichu is draped about the shoulders and pinned by Mrs. Adams' own gold and pearl hair brooch. The sequin-spangled fan and yellow slippers were also owned and used by her.

600. Shown in the East Room of the White House are, from right to left, Florence Kling Harding, Grace Goodhue Coolidge, Lou Henry Hoover, Anna Eleanor Roosevelt, Bess Wallace Truman, Mamie Doud Eisenhower, and Jacqueline Bouvier Kennedy.

601. Mrs. Johnson wears the antique gold satin gown she wore at a state dinner at the White House in honor of Prime Minister Harold Wilson of Great Britain on December 7, 1964. The gown has a matching satin stole.

597

598

599

600

601

602

603

604

602. Andrew Johnson's wife was an invalid when he became President at the death of Lincoln. Thus his eldest daughter, Martha Johnson Patterson, filled the position of First Lady. No dress of hers was available, but she wore this cloak while mistress of the White House. This Arab mantle made of silk and finely woven goat's hair was a stylish garment of the period for theater wear. The dress, one of the Museum's collection of period costumes, is of silk damask.

603. The traditional white of the satin wedding dress of Sarah Yorke Jackson, wife of President Andrew Jackson's adopted son, has mellowed to a soft ivory over the years. The skirt is of white mull, with panels of a flower design in satin stitch.

604. The mannequin of Mrs. Lincoln wears her watch-bracelet of blue enamel set with diamond chips. The octagonal shaped watch is 1⅜ inches long.

605. The Victorian Parlor of the White House represents
the years 1845 to 1869. From left to right are Betty Taylor Bliss,
Abigail Powers Fillmore, Jane Appleton Pierce, Harriet Lane,
niece of President James Buchanan, Mary Todd Lincoln,
and, at the right, Martha Johnson Patterson.
The wallpaper is copied from a small piece found under
several layers of plaster and paneling during the recent
renovation. The heavily carved laminated rosewood furniture
made by John Belter is typical of that found in fashionable
American homes of the period.

Abigail Powers Fillmore wears a simple lavender taffeta
dress which has a boned and laced bodice, fashionable at the
time. Popular at the time also was the handkerchief ring,
such as the one from which her lace handkerchief hangs.

Harriet Lane is shown in the dress she wore when she
married Henry Elliott Johnson of Baltimore. It is of white moire
taffeta, now mellowed with age to a deep ivory, with a tight
fitting, deeply pointed bodice of net, satin, and lace. Her
beautiful bridal veil of point lace is draped in the semblance
of a shawl, complementing the dress. The very full skirt
has a shallow train.

606

606. Jacqueline Kennedy's inaugural ball gown is of white peau d'ange veiled with chiffon. The transparent overblouse covers a collarless, sleeveless fitted bodice embroidered with metallic silver and brilliants. The floor length cape is of matching silk.

607. John Quincy Adams used the set of which this plate is a piece as state china. According to family tradition, he bought the set in France while Minister to Russia.

608. These pieces of Chinese export porcelain were owned by the Washingtons.

609. The Lowestoft two handled cup belonged to Mrs. Washington.

610. The Chinese export water bottle was used by George Washington.

611. The people of Paris presented this Lalique glass pin to the second Mrs. Woodrow Wilson when she accompanied her husband to Europe in 1919 for the Peace Conference.

612. Mrs. Lincoln's mourning watch is set in black onyx.

607

608

609

610

612

611

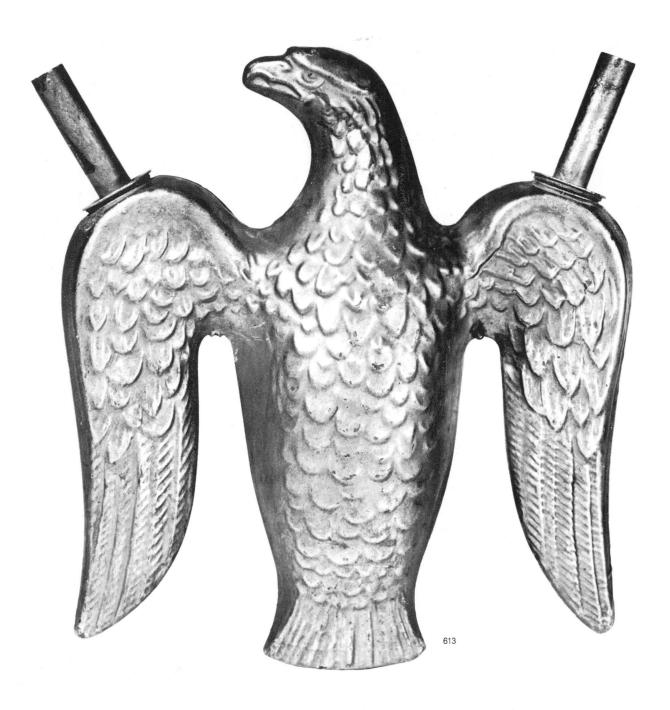

613

HISTORIC AMERICANS

ONE EVERCHANGING FACET of American life is the world of politics. Memorabilia of famous figures who have been leaders in the political life of the United States and items which characterized the political campaigns since the first major one in 1840 are shown in the exhibition entitled "Historic Americans."

Political campaigns have changed greatly since the first ones waged successfully by John Adams and Thomas Jefferson. (George Washington was unopposed and unanimously elected.) The man who became the second President of the United States conducted his campaign over a glass of sherry in his own elegantly appointed parlor or in the homes of the nation's leading citizens.

614

615

613. The double torch in the shape of an eagle was held high on a wooden pole.

614. The log cabin appears on this 1840 campaign spoon.

615. Campaign materials range from elaborately decorated pitchers to straw hats. Shown in detail is an Abe Lincoln campaign ribbon of 1860.

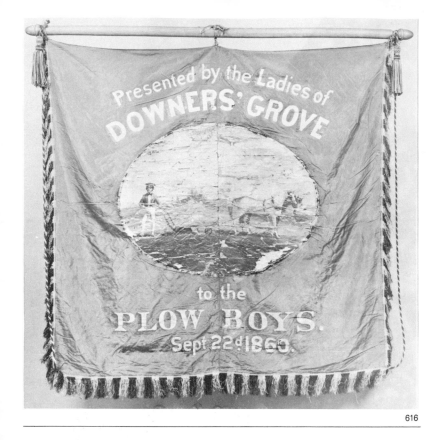

616

616, 617. Typical campaign banners were decorated with slogans and the images of the candidates.

618. With the Benjamin Harrison log cabin headquarters as its beginning, a typical torchlight parade, with uniformed marchers carrying banners, torches, and other paraphernalia, represents no one campaign but is a composite of many between the years 1840 and 1910.

619. The Buffalo, New York, delegation of the Central Italian Republican Club is shown with President McKinley in front of his porch.

618

619

E.PLURIBUS UNUM.

FOR

HARRISON & TYLER,

And no reduction of the prices of labour.

THE LOG CABIN,

The house our fathers lived in.

STONEHAM

JULY 4, 1840.

617

CLAY AND FRELINGHUYSEN

UNIFORM BANK CURRENCY
REVENUE ON IMPORTS
PROTECTION OF AMERICAN INDUSTRY
DISTRIBUTION OF THE PROCEEDS OF
THE PUBLIC LANDS AMONG THE STATES
ONE PRESIDENTIAL TERM
REDUCTION OF EXECUTIVE POWER.

620

THE WHIGS OF OLD WASHINGTON
WILL STAND BY THE UNION

621

THE ADAMS FAMILY

622

623

624

627

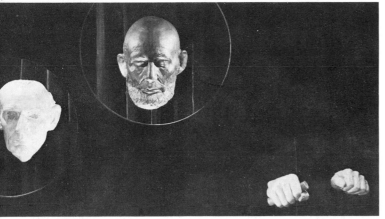

625

626

620. Henry Clay, often a candidate but never President, is pictured on a campaign banner.

621. The Whigs used George Washington as a symbol on their banner.

622. The doll, lace wedding veil, jewelry, and ceramic figurines were used by the Adams family.

623. Engraving from *Harper's Weekly* shows typical torchlight parade of the Lincoln-Hamlin campaign in 1860.

624. A log cabin is prominently worked into an appliquéd quilt of the period.

625. The life cast on the left was made of Lincoln's face in April, 1860; the one on the right in February, 1865. The stick in the life cast of Lincoln's right hand is a piece of a broomstick cut and held by him at the time of the casting.

626. President Grant was painted wearing his uniform as General of the United States Army in this family portrait by William Cogswell.

627. Shown is a reconstruction of Ford's first gas engine, 1893.

243

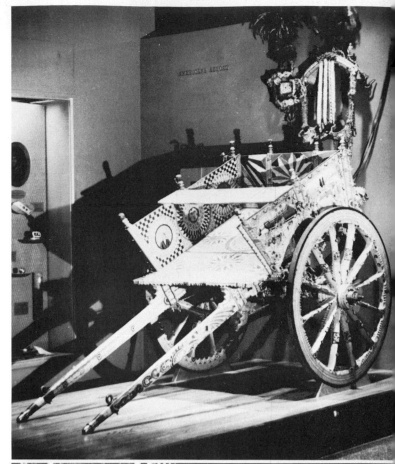

628. General of the Army George C. Marshall was presented with this Sicilian cart in 1951 as a token of appreciation for the contribution made by America to Italy through the European Recovery Plan. The plumed trappings for the donkey hang above the cart. On one side of the cart are the portraits of General Marshall and President Truman.

629. The box contains samples of several types of cables used by Cyrus Field in laying the Atlantic cable.

630. On the morning after the inauguration of President Kennedy, Robert Frost presented the Smithsonian Institution with the manuscript in his own hand of the poem ''The Gift Outright'' which he had recited as part of the inaugural ceremonies.

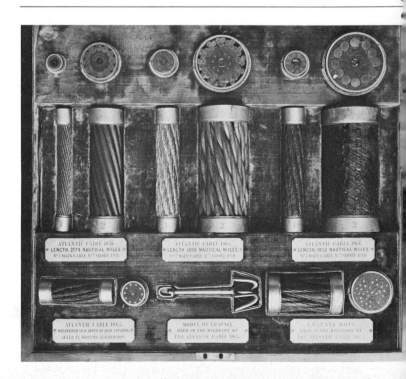

The Gift Outright

The land was ours before we were the land's
She was our land more than a hundred years
Before we were her people. She was ours
In Massachusetts in Virginia
But we were England's, still colonials,
Possessing what we still were unpossessed by,
Possessed by what we now no more possessed.
Something we were withholding made us weak
Until we found out that it was ourselves
We were withholding from our land of living
And forthwith found salvation in surrender.
Such as we were we gave ourselves outright
(The deed of gift was many deeds of war)
To the land vaguely realizing westward,
But still unstoried artless unenhanced
Such as she was such as she would become

                                    Robert Frost

For the Inauguration
of John F. Kennedy.

1961   To the Smithsonian

COSTUME

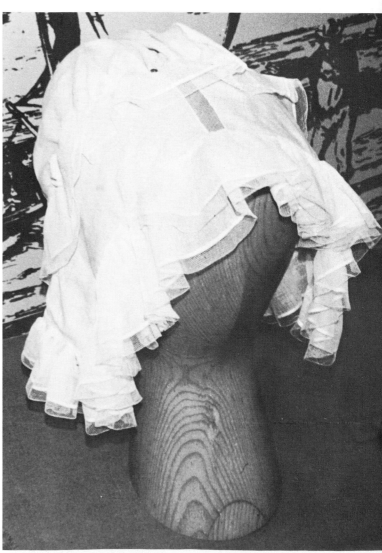

Throughout history clothing has been much more than just a protection from the elements. Rank, religious beliefs, social status, profession, age, and sex have dictated an individual's attire. Much of the history of a nation is written in the costumes its citizens have worn.

633

634

635   636

631. The young woman looking at herself in the mirror is wearing an 1880 satin brocade wedding gown.

632. Colonial America was greatly influenced by fashions and styles popular in Europe, as shown in this eighteenth century American mobcap, a style worn by ladies on both sides of the ocean.

633. Often in the Eighteenth century a young man apprenticed himself to an established craftsman for a certain number of years. Upon completing his apprenticeship he was given a "Freedom Suit" such as this linen-lined one given in 1775 to Jonathan Sheldon by John Townsend of Newport, Rhode Island.

634. Typical of the 1840's was this dress of barege—silk and cotton gauze—with chiné flower design.

635. The scarlet cloak was in high favor in eighteenth century America. This cardinal or hooded cloak is trimmed with shag, a kind of cloth of wool and goat's or camel's hair.

636. Sarah Pierpont wore this dress of lampas when she married Jonathan Edwards in 1727. It was later remodeled for her daughter, Mary Edwards, when she married Timothy Dwight.

637. The Empire styles of Europe influenced American dress of the early nineteenth century. The white dimity dress on the left was worn about 1800, the dress of grenadine next to it was worn in New York about 1820. The man's costume consists of a wool-brocade coat and linen pantaloons, worn in Maryland. The little boy wears a handwoven cotton suit, and the little girl a linen dress. On the right is a child's dress of silk crepe of about 1819.

638. This handmade corset was worn at Natchez, Mississippi, in 1820.

639. A hoop was worn under this 1855 silk dress.

640. Femininity was the key note of the turn of the century, with the new corset of 1901-02 giving the figure the S curve silhouette so typical of the period. Lace was the most popular fabric of the time. This silk chiffon two-piece dress is trimmed with Chantilly lace.

641. Skirts were higher in the early 1920's as shown by the velvet evening gown on the right. Inserts create an uneven hemline on the 1929 georgette crepe evening gown, left, forecasting the longer skirts to come.

642. The 1958 dress by Christian Dior is lined with black silk organza. On the right is a two-piece wool dress of 1959, by Norman Norell.

641

642

643

HISTORY OF THE ARMED FORCES

644

SINCE BEFORE THE Revolution, the courage and prowess of the American fighting man have been legendary. Illustrated by drawings of the fighting men themselves in the uniforms they wore, one of the largest exhibits in the Museum of History and Technology tells the story of the American soldier, sailor, marine, coast guardsman, and airman, with his weapons and equipment, uniforms and decorations giving a detailed picture of the conditions under which he lived and fought.

One impressive exhibit is the Continental gundelo *Philadelphia*, an American vessel sunk by the British October 11, 1776, during the Battle of Valcour Island. When this gunboat was discovered in 1935, her white pine mast was still standing upright, its top barely ten feet below the surface of Valcour Bay. Displayed in her entirety, the *Philadelphia* once again has her twelve-pound bow guns, nine-pound broadside guns, one-pound swivel guns, and her anchors in place. A raised viewing platform permits the interior of the gundelo to be seen, with the brick fireplace, a kettle, frying pan, and chopping block nearby. This sunken vessel, which lay at the bottom of Lake Champlain in New York for over a century and a half, is fifty-seven feet long and has a sixteen foot beam. The twenty-four pound shot, marked with the English Crown's "broad arrow," which shattered her planks and frames at one point, caused the rapid flooding that compelled her crew to abandon her. The shot is displayed at the point at which it hit the vessel. **(643, 644.)**

645

646

645. Adam Stephen, a lieutenant colonel in the British colonial forces during the French and Indian War, wore this waistcoat, around 1755.

646. This uniform coat was worn by Peter Gansevoort as a colonel of the New York State militia about 1777.

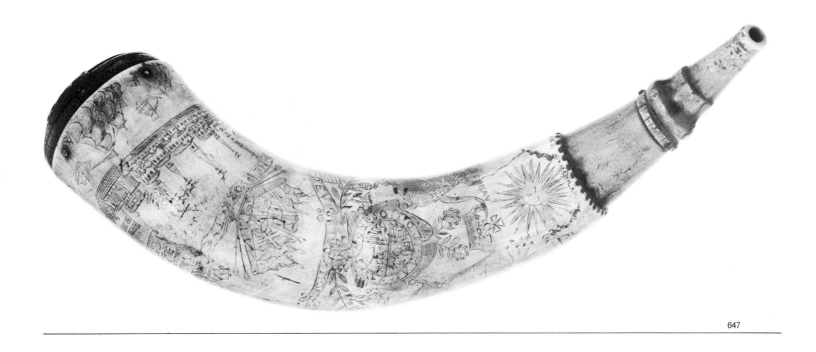

647. With hand carving of the British coat-of-arms and a map of what is now part of New York state, this powder horn is inscribed, "This horn made by Samuel Davis at Fort Ontario September 23, 1762."

648. Baron de Kalb's saddle.

649. During the War of 1812 this kettledrum was captured from the British 21st Foot Royal Scots Fusileers by the American forces.

650. The Revolutionary War mess kit was used by George Washington.

649

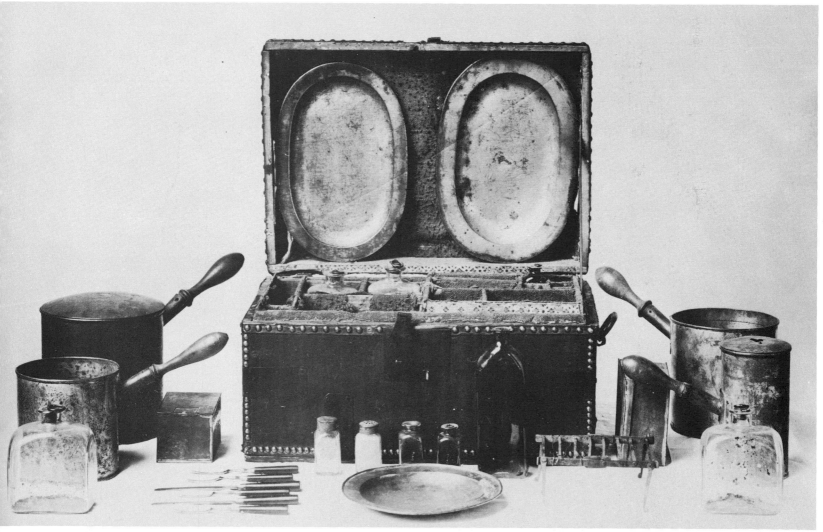

650

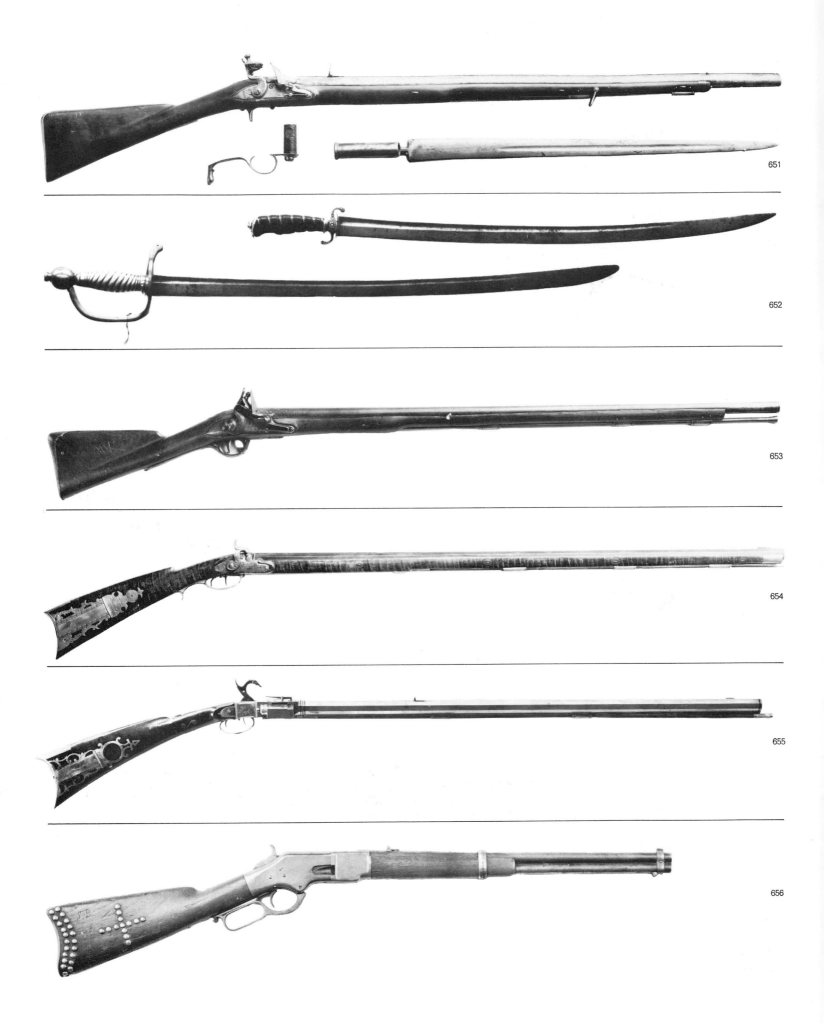

651

652

653

654

655

656

254

651. In the late eighteenth century Major Patrick Ferguson, a British officer during the American Revolution, invented this breechloader which did not require removal of the screw plug. He fired six rounds at a 200-yard target in one minute to demonstrate his rifle. He presented it to his second-in-command, Captain Frederick de Peyster.

652. On November 10, 1775, the Continental Congress ordered the organization of two battalions of marines for service on ships of the Continental Navy. Shown is a marine officer's sword. Below it a noncommissioned officer's sword.

653. The marines used flintlock muskets of the type of the "Brown Bess."

654. Swiss and German settlers in Pennsylvania altered the massive jaeger rifle to suit the new conditions for hunting and warfare found in the New World. Lighter, long-barreled, and more accurate, this rifle was first known as the Pennsylvania rifle. Later it achieved fame as the Kentucky rifle because of its use by Daniel Boone and other frontiersmen.

655. Sam Houston owned this "Harmonica" rifle.

656. One of the most famous rifles is the Winchester. This one is dated 1873.

657. The saber was a dragoon saber of the War of 1812.

658. The single shot U.S. pistol was later used by Mexicans.

657

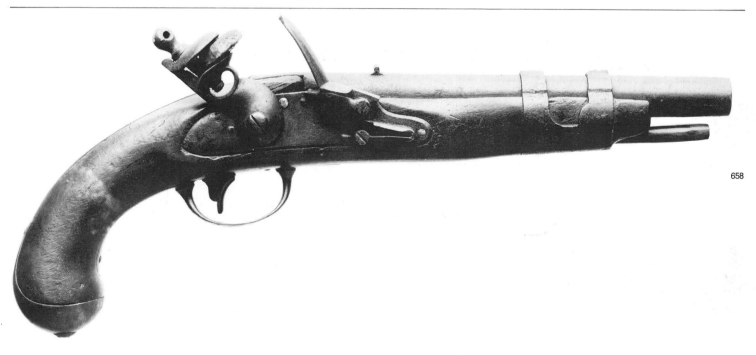

658

659

660

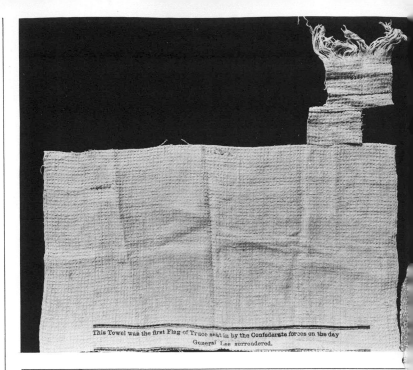

This Towel was the first Flag of Truce sent in by the Confederate forces on the day General Lee surrendered.

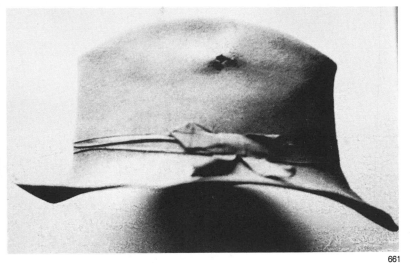

661

662

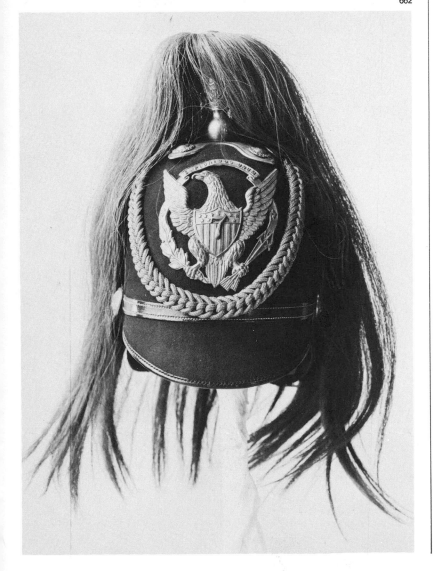

659. The dragoon helmet is dated 1812.

660. The dragoon cap was used in 1835.

661. The cavalry campaign hat is of the Spanish-American War period.

662. The United States 7th Regiment cavalry dress helmet was worn in the late nineteenth century.

663. The towel that was the first flag of truce sent in by the Confederate forces on the day General Lee surrendered.

664. This pair of shoes belonged to a Confederate soldier.

665, 666. This officer's camp kit was among his personal belongings. It is shown both closed and open.

665

666

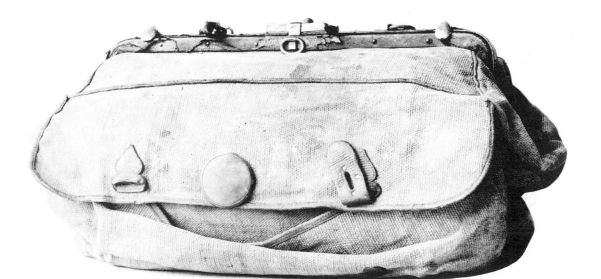

667

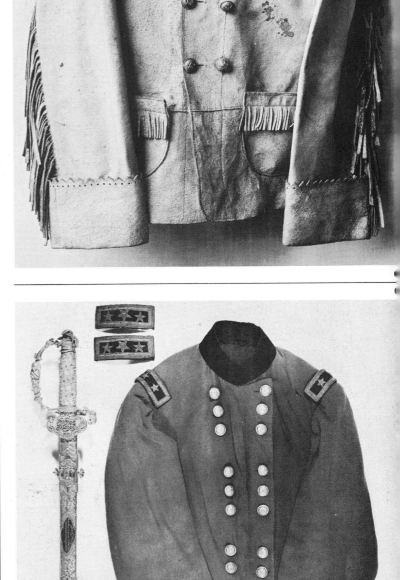

667. The hatchet inscribed with his name was owned by Davy Crockett.

668. The nameplate of the U.S.S. *Maine* recalled the battle of Manila Bay in the Spanish-American War.

669. General Custer wore this buckskin coat in the 1870's.

670. This uniform and presentation sword belonged to General McClellan.

671. The shock weapon of World War I was the armored tank. One of the original tanks of that war was this six-ton United States tank, model 1917.

672. Mounted on the stern of a merchant ship, this five-inch naval gun may have fired the first American shot of World War I.

668

671

672

259

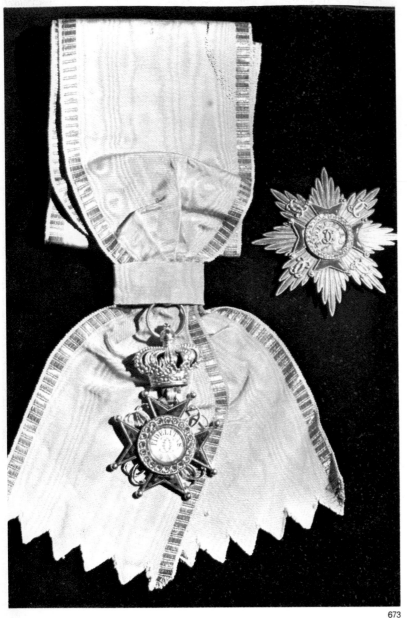

673

674

675

ILLUMINATED MANUSCRIPTS and paintings of the Crusaders show them with banners and shields emblazoned with heraldic devices. These colorful symbols have come down through the ages in the form of the Orders awarded by many sovereigns to worthy subjects.

The custom of awarding decorations for meritorious service is continued with military orders, decorations, and insignia. Philosophic, scientific, and other organizations have honored outstanding achievements in their respective fields by the presentation of medals or similar awards.

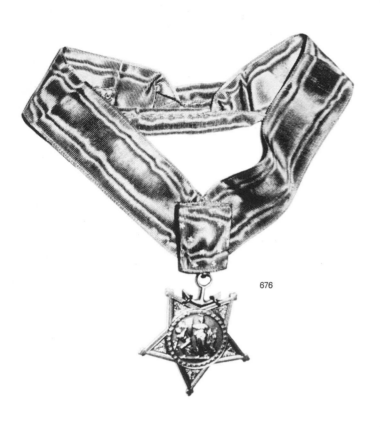

ORDERS, MEDALS AND DECORATIONS

673. The Order of Fidelity was also used in Baden.

674. The Order of Berthold, founded by Duke Friedrich of Baden in 1877.

675. The Order of the Star of Nepal, founded in 1947.

676. The Medal of Honor is the highest decoration awarded by the United States.

677. One of Great Britain's orders is the Order of St. Patrick. This one was formerly owned by the Earl of Dudley, 1902.

678. The Order of Malta, founded in Jerusalem in 1048 and established in Spain in 1602.

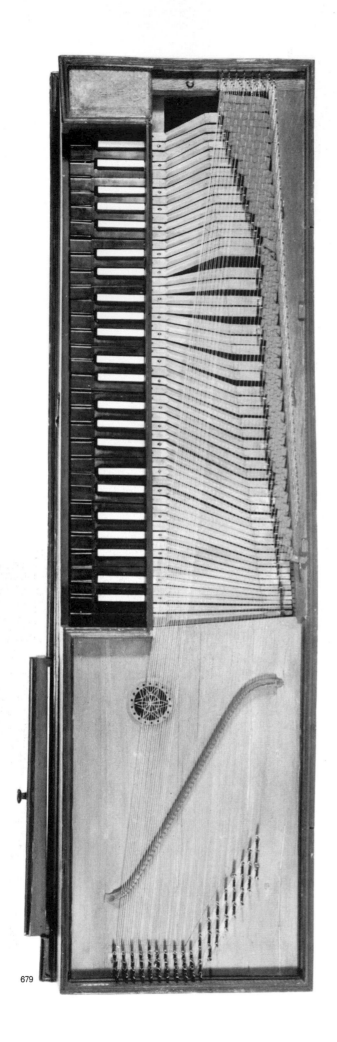

679

MUSICAL INSTRUMENTS

A MUSICAL INSTRUMENT does not lend itself well to being sealed up in a museum case. Not only does it have to be played regularly to keep its interior workings from deteriorating, it does not come alive until it can be heard. A small concert stage in the Museum of History and Technology's exhibition of musical instruments makes possible periodic recitals and more frequent demonstrations of the instruments, both foreign made and American, in the collection.

679. The spacing of the keys shows that this eighteenth century German instrument is a fretted clavicord, the frets making it possible to have more keys than the number of strings.

680. This clavicord was used by the Moravians at their religious meetings in the United States in the nineteenth century.

681. Mozart played a grand piano made by Johann Andreas Stein of Augsburg, Germany, who made this grand piano in 1773.

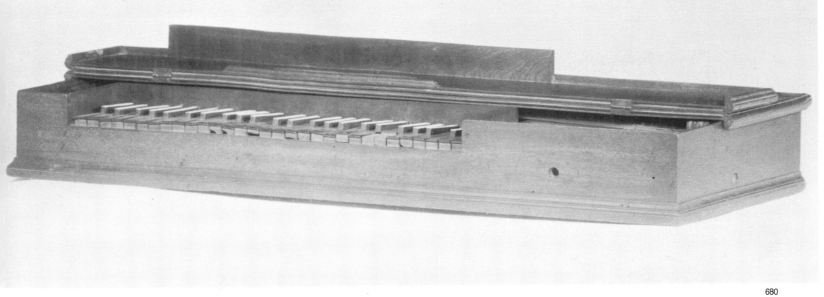

682. This pipe organ, dated at the turn of the nineteenth century, is probably of American make although it is in the English style.

683. Although made up of parts of older instruments, this music box is as it was when the Smithsonian received it in 1882. The musical movement was probably made about 1880 by Bremond, a Swiss.

684. Barnum's famous midget Tom Thumb used this miniature grand piano on his exhibition tours. Approximately four feet long, it was made in 1851 by Kirkman and Son of London and exhibited at the London Crystal Palace Exhibition.

685. Over-the-shoulder horns were used in the 1860's by marching band musicians. The horns directed the sound back toward the marchers behind them. These over-the-shoulder saxhorns range from the small soprano saxhorn to the large bass saxhorn.

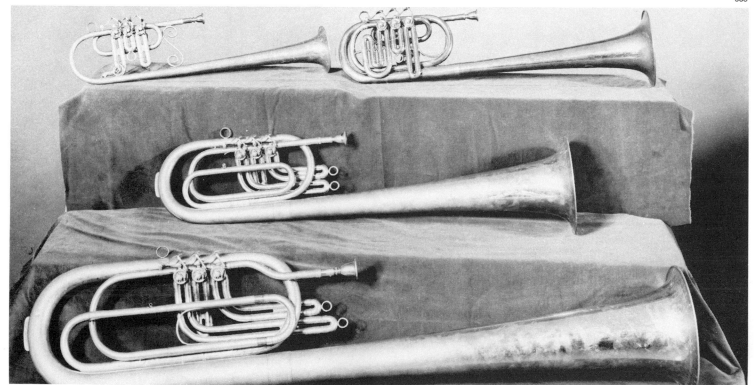

DURING THE ONE HUNDRED and twenty years of its existence, the Smithsonian Institution has never stood still. The second half of the twentieth century finds the institution traveling faster than ever toward many goals. Paramount in the future plans is the great new John F. Kennedy Center for the Performing Arts. The building, designed by Edward Durrell Stone, is fast becoming a reality, with the new department being assembled to evolve and develop ideas as to how the center can best serve the American people.

Another major program is the preparation of many new exhibition halls in both the Museum of History and Technology and the Museum of Natural History.

One of the most ambitious of these new projects is a complex of galleries that, when complete, will tell the story of the development of the United States from the period of discovery to the present-day space age. Objects from all the collections in the Museum of History and Technology will be grouped together to show their interdependence and their relationship to each other and to the Americans who lived with them. An early costume will be shown near a textile machine of the same period and also in relation to a carriage of the type that the costume might have been worn in. A two-story Colonial house of the early 1700's will be shown in construction, with the figures of carpenters and bricklayers using the type tools with which it was originally constructed. The United States' growth from a backwoods colony to a leader in the Nuclear Age will be illustrated with authentic objects of the quality, scope, and variety that only the extensive collections of the Smithsonian Institution could make possible.

A second project planned for the Museum of History and Technology will bring the story of power up to date. In the past, America has been powered by water, the horse, steam, and gasoline, all covered by exhibits already completed. The power of the future is nuclear energy. The story of the major experiments that have advanced our knowledge of the structure and final practicality of splitting the atom, will be told with originals and replicas of apparatus used by Ernest Rutherford, J. J. Thompson, Enrico Fermi, and others. Ernest Lawrence's cyclotron will be shown. The first controlled nuclear fission observed by Fermi in 1942 will be commemorated by a reconstruction of his first atomic pile built at the University of Chicago, using some of the original materials.

The full size demonstration of the Figure-8 Stellarator, an early device by Lyman Spitzer, is already on display and symbolizes the energy source of the future.

Plans are being drawn to install a two thousand square foot walk-through replica of a tropical rain forest in the Hall of Botany. A Smithsonian Institution expedition recently returned from British Guiana where, at the foot of Kaieteur Falls in the Eataro River, scientists and preparators studied the plants and trees of the area. They are now at work fabricating this tremendous exhibit.

Full-scale representation of a tropical coral reef is under construction. Color photographs by Kjell Sandved, taken of living organisms found among the reefs of Puerto Rico and Hawaii, serve as models for the artists who are making realistic undersea creatures of wax and plastic for the exhibit.

Later on, exhibitions of mollusks and insects may exhibit color photographs showing the eye of a bee and the beauty of a butterfly's wing as they have never been seen before.

These projects and many others will be available for the Smithsonian visitor of a decade or two from now, as the Institution shares more and more of its treasures with the American people and the world.

PLANS AND PROGNOSTICATIONS

686

687

686. The architect's rendering of The National Cultural Center.

687. Built in two sections, the older portion of this Colonial house from Ipswich, Massachusetts, is from the 1690's. The newer section was built about 1752. Shown being installed in the museum, the house will be exhibited as though in construction. Photograph by John William Brown.

688. Given by President John F. Kennedy, this atlas of 1692 by Nicolas Sanson of Paris is entitled *Nouvelle Introduction à la Géographie pour Monseigneur le Dauphin.*

688

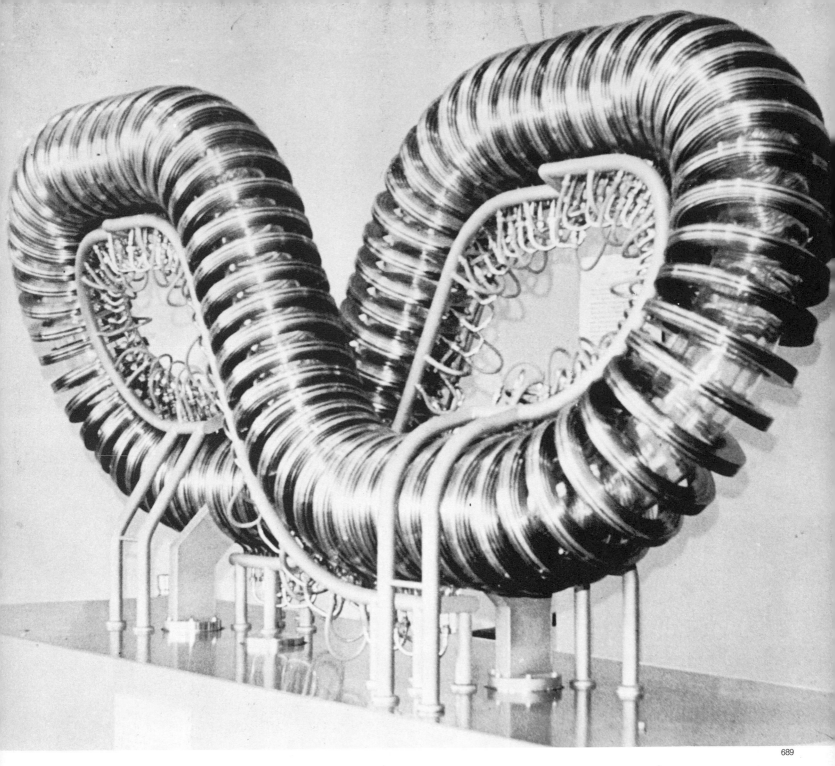

689

690

691

692

693

694

695

696

689. The figure-eight stellarator, shown by this full size demonstration model, was made by Lyman Spitzer.

690. The carrousel figure of the sea horse is from the Mabel and Eleanor Van Alstyne Folk Art Collection.

691. For the Hall of Botany. *Epidendrum ciliare*, an orchid found in Central America.

692. A top shell, *Clanculus rarus*, from the Seychelle Islands.

693. Breathing gills of the tube worm, *Polychaete annelid*, from Puerto Rico.

694. *Calliactis tricolor*, a Pacific anemone.

695. *Hermissenda crassicornus nudibranch*, from the Pacific coast of the United States.

696. For the Hall of Insects, eye of the horsefly, *Tobanid*.

INDEX